D0852617

JUST HARVEST

Just Harvest:
The Story of How Black Farmers Won the Largest Civil Rights Case
Against the U.S. Government

Copyright © 2021 by Gregorio A. Francis
All rights reserved.

No part of this book shall be reproduced or transmitted in any form or by any means, electronic, mechanical, magnetic, and photographic, including photocopying, recording or by information storage and retrieval system, without prior written permission of the publisher.

No patent liability is assumed with respect to the use of the information contained herein. Although every precaution has been taken in the preparation of this book, the publisher and author assume no responsibility for errors and omissions. Neither is any liability assumed for damages resulting from the use of information contained herein.

Published by Forefront Books.

Cover Design by Bruce Gore, Gore Studio Inc.
Interior Design by Bill Kersey, Kersey Graphics

ISBN: 978-1-948677-80-6
ISBN: 978-1-948677-81-3 (e-Book)

JUST HARVEST

THE STORY
of How Black Farmers
Won the Largest Civil Rights Case
Against the U.S. Government

GREG A. FRANCIS

Forefront
BOOKS

TABLE OF CONTENTS

Part Three: A Sense of Justice

ACKNOWLEDGMENTS

I WOULD FIRST LIKE TO THANK AND ACKNOWLEDGE THE HAND OF God in my life. I know that I have been put in places and been allowed to have certain experiences only by His grace, and I want to acknowledge and thank Him for that.

Next, I would like to thank my parents.

To my mother, Annette Thompson: You are a force of nature. Your determination, love, and encouragement throughout the years has meant everything to me. As the song lyrics go, "You are the wind beneath my wings."

To my stepfather, John Thompson, who has now passed: They say that fatherhood is a job with delayed gratification. Thank you for taking on that effort and that commitment. Thank you also for being a strict disciplinarian. I hated "squaring" my room away; however, now I recognize that you were merely teaching me discipline and order, which has been important to me throughout my life.

To my late dad, Enoes Francis: Thank you always loving me and sacrificing your happiness for mine. You are greatly missed and thought of often.

To my deceased grandmother and grandfather, who gave me vision, and who had big dreams for me and all of the members of their family: Your encouragement, your examples, and your prayers are certainly appreciated.

To my wife, Keisha: Your undying love and commitment to me and to our family is unmatched. I thank you for your encouragement. I thank you for challenging me. But most of all, I thank you for the support and care that you give our children.

To Grier and Rio: You are my reason for being. You are my muses in life. Everything I do is for you and I hope this book is a constant reminder of my commitment to you, but also of the commitment that you have to society to do good in your lifetime.

To my sisters, Pamela, Kathia, and Kimberly: Thank you for all your love and support. I know that I have three warriors in my corner at any moment in time and I appreciate you being there for me.

To H. Scott Bates, my former law partner, friend, and mentor: I thank you for your commitment to me and your belief in my vision. When things got difficult or weren't necessarily going my way—and when others had their doubts—you encouraged and supported me. Most of all, you allowed me to finish this project in a way that has forever changed my life.

To Angelia: Thank you for being present. Present for the highs and lows, for the strategy sessions, for the consternations, and ultimately, resolution. Your loyalty and dedication not only to this project, but to my vision of what a lawyer and law firm should be, have been critical to my success.

To John Morgan, my former partner: Thank you for the "STAGE," the opportunities will never be forgotten. Thank you to Scott Weinstein and Andrew Meyer, my former partners; your legal brilliance and brief writing abilities assured us a spot at the table. No one saw us coming.

To Mike Espy, who is really responsible for this historic event: You are a selfless man, surely ahead of your time. Thank you for working with me and giving me advice in this case and in life.

To Mark Hayes: You were a complete pain in my ass throughout this editorial process, but I thank you for your encouragement, for your vision, and for your commitment to the success of this project and my law firm. And to Jason Schmidt and the entire team at Platform Creators, thank you for your dedicated work and creativity which continues to amaze me.

To my law partner, Joe Osborne: You gave me an opportunity when opportunities were scarce. You chose me to be a member of a law firm, not knowing that 25 years after completing my summer clerkship there we would begin another journey together as partners in this crusade to serve the underserved and to speak for those who cannot speak for themselves. I love you, brother.

To Hank Sanders, co-lead counsel in this case and my mentor: You are an example of exactly what is meant when it is said, "God will put people in your lives at the right time and the right place." Your words of encouragement, your restoration of history, what you have been through on your journey to become a lawyer, and in all your work to serve your community have taught me to be a better person, a better lawyer, and a better man. You helped me to understand the commitment I have—and that we *all* have as lawyers—to pursue justice. And to his lovely wife, Rose, who provided me with perspective and encouragement.

To Andy Marks, co-lead counsel in this case: Thank you for your example, for your commitment to the farmers, and for seeking justice. Your determination to see those who are underserved or underrepresented, or who have no voice, has been tremendous, and I thank you for continuing to work with me and Hank in finding further solutions for Black farmers.

To Jim Farin and Eric Sanchez: Eric, Jim, you brought order and discipline to the case and a commitment to seeing it through to the end. Thank you for your partnership, for your dedication, and for bringing this case to a successful resolution. And to the mad scientist in you, Eric, thank you for all the numbers work and the research you did. Your efforts were integral to the success of this case. Your evaluation of where the potential claimants were, and when and where we should hold the various meetings, were key to ensuring that the most eligible participants had an opportunity to have legal advice in filing their claims.

To my best friend, Renaldo Garcia: Thank you for your belief in me and your confidence in my ability to get ahead and to do well. Thank you, too, for the use of your vehicle throughout law school to get me back and forth to class. I know it was a sacrifice for you then; however, you never complained or mentioned it. You have my gratitude.

To my friend Tony Glover, whom I have known from childhood and who has been with me at every significant step I've taken in my career: Thank you for your commitment. Thank you for your willingness to believe in me. And thank you for your support of me. I hope to provide the same for you.

Thank you to Omar Nelson, Chris Espy, Abraham Gates, and Courtney Cockrell: Your hard work, dedication, and commitment to seeing that the farmers who have been aggrieved were given the best opportunity to present their case. Your investment of time, effort, and passion made all the difference in this case.

Thank you to Willard Tillman: Your work in Oklahoma is unmatched when it comes to advocating for Black farmers.

Thank you to Alva Waller and Stephen Carpenter who served as the ombudsmans in this case: You held our feet to the fire on behalf of the farmers and made sure that we performed as lawyers should. I am grateful for that commitment, and I thank you for your words of encouragement and advice along the way. Alva, although we're the same age, you truly are my big sister.

To Delano Stewart, who took me under his wing and continues to check on me today: Your example as a lawyer, as a friend, and as a father have meant the world to me.

To James Wade: I miss you so. Thank you for all of the advice that you have given me, for believing in me, and for ensuring that I truly believed in myself. I wish we had more time together, but I value and thank you for the time that we did have together.

Special thanks also go to my publisher, Jonathan Merkh at Forefront Books, for his keen interest in and support of this book; to my collaborators and researchers and their dedicated support and for the tireless hours they spent on these pages and their meticulous attention to detail; and to my editor Hope Innelli for the added care she gave to this work. Thank you for helping me tell this story to the world.

And, most of all, thank you to the tens of thousands of Black farmers who entrusted us with their message and livelihoods after fighting the good fight on their own for so long. Your resilience, determination, and faith will remain with me forever.

FOREWORD

"This has been their plight: to live in the richest nation
on earth, amidst some of the most fertile soil on the planet,
and not have enough to eat, not be able to feed their families,
and not for want of trying."[1]

I T'S NOT FOR WANT OF TRYING.

Since Abraham Lincoln founded the Department of Agriculture in 1862, branding it as "the People's Department," the Black farmer in America has been trying to seek inclusion as full partner in President Lincoln's mid-19th century governmental experiment.

And during the Depression era, when the USDA widely expanded its authority in order to keep majority producers afloat, becoming in essence, the "lender of last resort," the African-American farmer again and again found himself at the opposite end of the turn row.

And yet today, as the United States Department of Agriculture has grown over the decades into a 21st-century behemoth, with 120 billion dollar's worth of programs and policies, the Black farmer has to fight for recognition, respect, and for literal restitution.

Growing up Black in Mississippi, I am no stranger to Jim Crow and institutional discrimination. I grew up around, below, and within the system. And although I was never a farmer, I remember the tales of administrative discrimination that my father used to tell from his experiences as the first "Negro" County Extension Agent in Crittenton County, Arkansas, in the 1940s. My father studied agriculture at the knee of renowned professor Dr. George Washington Carver of Tuskegee Institute.

In January 1993, the first day I sat at the desk in my cavernous office as Secretary of Agriculture, a young staffer went to the basement vault and unearthed my father's notes as the USDA County Extension Agent.

As I opened the timeworn manila envelope and began to read, I shuddered. His notes chronicled wrongful episodes of mistreatment, rejection, and rank racism against his impoverished Black farmer clients. He copiously described how federal resources were diverted, how needed loans were denied, and how loan applications were dismissively thrown into the trash.

I shuddered in anticipation because power in Washington had changed, and now we were the people empowered to bring reform. Cloaked with the awesome authority as Secretary of Agriculture and knowing that I had the approval of the Clinton administration regarding our intentions toward changing the way government worked, I believed that fundamental and equitable reforms were on the way.

We set out to change the structure, approach, and outreach of the USDA, which was known as "the last plantation." Our aim was to transform that federal agency into one that would fully appreciate the contributions of all of its customers, patrons, and beneficiaries—regardless of race, gender, age, or small-producer classification.

We soon found that, alas, change comes about very slowly to an aged behemoth.

However, there is good news. When two branches of government, the Executive and Legislative, can't get it done, our nation allows the option to aggressively engage the third, the Judiciary, for redress. And in order to have success before the courts you have to have capable, talented, and indefatigable advocates.

The book that follows is all about such a successful effort, and that talented and prodigious advocate is my friend, Greg Francis. Greg led other great lawyers in petitioning the federal courts on behalf of a large class of African-American farmers, and achieved landmark success—the largest civil rights settlement in the history of the United States.

It was not easy. The USDA behemoth had to be corralled, and the Justice Department had to be convinced that the financial losses were real, that the systemic discrimination was certifiable, and that the consequential damages were continuing.

Just Harvest: The Story of How Black Farmers Won the Largest Civil Rights Case Against the U.S. Government deserves the attention of all who want to learn the tactics and techniques of valuating generational inequality, convincing the recalcitrant agencies to pay, and then how to actually wrest payment from the bureaucracy.

Because of Greg Francis and his colleagues, something remarkable occurred. On the same day in America, thousands of Black farmers received a check in the mail from the United States Treasury Department for $50,000 each—1.2 billion dollars in total—a long overdue apology for generations of scorn, dismissal, and wanton discrimination.

Fifty thousand dollars won't rebuild a flagging farm operation, but since this landmark settlement the USDA has demonstrated its willingness to reach out assiduously to African-American and small stakeholder farmers.

We know that more needs to be done. African-American farmers need access to credit, technical assistance and to training. They need loan forgiveness, bankruptcy forbearance, and equitable inclusion in the full panoply of the USDA's programs. They need and demand respect and recognition. Because of Greg and all of the other tireless advocates, inside and outside of USDA, they are getting it.

My father would have been proud.

Mike Espy
25th Secretary of Agriculture
Former Member of Congress

INTRODUCTION

Beware. This book is a jagged reality pill. If you take it, you will never be able to unknow the truth. The truth about what we are all capable of as a society and what you are liable for in its evolution. I hope this book brings out the best in you, to offset the evil that can be awakened in us all. This book reveals actual history, the realities of how tough it is to get justice, and one lawyer's account of how your identity impacts both.

Writing this introduction was more difficult than writing the book. The book is simply the story as I lived it. This introduction is why it matters to me that you read it and live it too. The experiences it conveys forever changed the way I practice law, raise my children, love my wife, and stay engaged in the community. I hope it inspires you likewise.

I am frequently asked how it feels to win the largest civil rights case in U.S. history. Most people think the settlement size ($1.25 billion) is what makes the case extraordinary. It is not. Not even close. People ask why it never made headline news the way the *Brown v. Board of Education* case did. I recently had another attorney tell me, "You're the most successful civil rights attorney in America that nobody knows."

I have thought about that, prayed, lost many nights of sleep, and the best explanation I can offer is that there is no glory in war. In the same way servicemen seldom talk about what they saw in battle, those who engaged in this one have remained similarly silent. I can tell you it was war for me. But my hell working this case was nothing compared to what I discovered happened to tens of thousands of Black families, their businesses, and their farms.

Rape is not a strong enough word for what happened to these farmers. For what happened to generations who had all too recently given their blood and sweat working to feed the very people who had for decades enslaved them. For what happened to working men, women, and children who were time and again stripped of all hope. Listening to story after story of how these farmers rose from slavery to build a foundation that could have helped erase much of the hatred for the very system that had kept them captive humbled and inspired me.

This is the story of stolen glory, of rising from the depths of slavery, empowering future generations to be self-supportive, creating jobs, earning the rights of entrepreneurial freedom, as well as being a source of healing past national crimes. This is the story of true tragedy—and worse, of a missed opportunity for the world to learn from it.

What was committed was not just an assault on Black farmers. It was an assault on capitalism, an assault on the American way of life, an assault fueled by organized evil. And what haunts me today is that unlike flat-out slavery, which I am sure will never happen in my lifetime, the atrocities inflicted by our own federal government can easily be re-established through stealthy government departments that can operate without oversight, creating opportunities for this hell to repeat itself.

The corruption, greed, and racism that these farmers endured is still alive. The government may have admitted guilt and wrote a check but that is not what these farmers wanted. They wanted to be heard. They wanted their stories to be told, they wanted to protect future generations, Black and White, from ever letting this happen again. I want to be clear: the moral of this story is not how to stop racism or revive the Black farming community. The moral of this story is how your individual identity, your beliefs about what you are capable of, and what you are responsible for, determine the level of justice we will have as a society.

History matters. In 1920 there were more than 925,000 Black farmers with families who had risen from slavery, becoming one of the most successful examples of entrepreneurialism this country has ever seen.[2] Black farmers owned over 16 million acres of farmland, about one-seventh of all farm operations in the U.S.[3] It has been estimated that as much as 30 percent of all food served on American tables back then came from Black-owned farms. But by the time this entrepreneurial genocide got my attention, Black farmers had been stripped of all but about one million acres to farm. Up until the point the federal government got involved, there seemed to be an air of cooperation between the farmers, both Black and White. Farming is an extremely hard life and there was a mutual respect between them. I will not go into the details here because it is so well documented in the book, but the entire reason the federal government got involved in farming in the first place was because of how successful American farmers had become and how meaningful, and yet fragile, the industry was to the overall economy. Farming is one of America's greatest examples of entrepreneurialism, collaboration, cooperation, innovation, and grit the world has ever seen. Unlike industries where strong iconic figures such as Henry Ford or the Wright Brothers were celebrated by the press, no one figure could represent the little guy, the hard-working American farmer who kept us all from going hungry. Thus, an opportunity for politicians and government agencies to exploit an industry to advance their own political agendas existed. The United States Department of Agriculture (USDA) did what most government agencies do. They created an infrastructure to facilitate the distribution of taxpayers' dollars in the form of expansion and operating loans for farmers. These loans were sold to the American people as a way to help American farmers stay solvent through tough times and to ensure that our food distribution capability was never in question.

The problems began when government employees (mostly non-farmers) were artificially empowered as "leaders" within the farming community. Armed with large sums of taxpayers' dollars, these bureaucrats were able to pick and choose which farmers received assistance. Bribery, corruption, and racism are the obvious sparks and flames of this national dumpster-fire, but there is an equally repulsive disorder we all have that enabled this entrepreneurial genocide to happen right under everyone's nose and to last for so long. The systemic racism exercised by "our" government was so pervasive, so blatant, so evil, that there was never even an attempt to prove that it did not happen, just the surrender of money for it. And again, with taxpayers' dollars. At times this book will make you sick. When you hear the stories that I heard, you will find yourself asking, *How can this happen? What can we do to stop it from happening again? Where are all these evil people?*

Better questions to ask yourself are, *What can I do?* and *How can we grow leaders who will never cower from the sacrifice God's justice demands?* Keep reading.

Many nights I fell to my knees crying over the stress these farmers were facing, the stress of navigating our own legal system, and the feelings of insecurity as I tried to convince myself this was not just some ideological fantasy where all evil is vanquished by superheroes. This is America; life is not fair, and God's greatest lessons are oftentimes brutal. I hope this book challenges you and expands your awareness of your capabilities. As I stated earlier, it took me a while to have clarity. I needed time to unhinge from the organized narrative that government bureaucracies, large law firms, and spineless cowards have perfected to calculate the value of a human's identity and dignity.

As you read this story, I hope you will begin to understand the value of personal identity; not the acknowledgement from others, but rather, the security, dignity, and empowerment that come from "accepting responsibility" for you and your family's role in life. Along this journey I discovered two types of people: those who knew they mattered and those who hadn't seriously contemplated the subject.

Consider the epic stories in which Harry Potter, Luke Skywalker, Black Panther, Superman, Neo, and Jesus are told that their life matters to all of humanity. We watch these characters struggle with the weight of discovering that their actions are more important than they are. As bystanders (so we think), we see how they are tormented and we gasp as we witness them grow weak from the battle, at times on the verge of giving up. We say under our breath, "You can't give up, don't you know what you are capable of, what you are responsible for?" If they only knew. I imagine most caterpillars question if their struggles and sacrifice will one day lead to them being able to fly. If they only knew. If *you* only knew.

All caterpillars can fly—and so can you. Mike Espy, Hank Sanders, John Boyd, and Gary Grant are among the characters in this tragic story that knew they could fly, and that their actions mattered more than they did. So did the Black farmers who refused to give up, who refused to be silenced, lawyers who stood with me when so many others were against me, and my family and friends who believed in me more than I believed in myself. I hope this book makes you tell yourself, your children, and those in your charge that you will *never* give up and that your identity is *never* defined by someone else. It is defined in direct proportion to what you accept responsibility for. The Black farmers in this story had accepted the responsibility of feeding your family. I hope when you finish reading these pages, you will accept the responsibility of never letting their story and history be forgotten. *Pigford v. Glickman*—and the follow-up case I led with Henry Sanders and Andrew H. Marks, commonly referred to as Pigford II—may have been settled, but the struggle of Black farmers, Black entrepreneurs, and Black leaders can never be taken for granted or relegated to the government to be managed—or to any other organization. If we aspire to be free from the unjust oppression of the past, we must build a nation of strong Black communities that include Black participants and leaders, a nation of strong Black-owned businesses, a nation of strong Black leaders, and a nation of strong Black families. But that will never happen until each of us accepts the responsibility of building a strong sense of personal identity. And that can only be viewed from a mirror.

My hope is the dreams of "entrepreneurial freedom" that those Black farmers fought for will never die and you will find the courage to replant the seeds that God has given all of us. For there is nothing sweeter or more fulfilling than a *Just Harvest*.

PART ONE

A SENSE OF SELF

CHAPTER ONE

HELL'S GORGE

Even as a young child, I had a tremendous understanding of the power of identity. At its very core, identity is how we define ourselves; how we want our friends, families, and colleagues to perceive us; and, in part, how others ultimately see us. Identity can be a powerful thing—probably more powerful than you even know. Some of my identity derives from the energy of my birthplace. From the people who inhabited it during my time there and well before me. From the lore of how they did the impossible. How they helped tame and harness the temperament of the sea to ensure safe passage for those passing through.

I grew up near the Pedro Miguel Locks of the Panama Canal during the late 1960s and early 1970s. My maternal grandmother, Muriel Burgess, worked as a seamstress, sewing clothes for her ten children and later for her many grandchildren, selling whatever she could to make extra money. We didn't have much as far as material possessions, but we had what we needed to survive.

My grandmother was a very strong-willed and opinionated woman who was fully committed to her family. I guess you have to be when you have so many children. She also had a tremendous sense of humor. After

I was married, she told my wife, "You know, I don't like to kiss." My wife responded, "Well, you had to like it a little because you have ten kids." This elicited a hearty laugh from my grandmother.

When I was four years old, I started attending a preschool near my grandparents' house. Teachers asked students to bring a towel from home to dry their hands before lunch and after using the restroom. We didn't have paper towels back then. Most kids brought simple white terry towels. Since my grandmother was a seamstress, she stenciled my name and a design onto a soft blue one.

"Take this towel because you're special," she told me. "You're special. That's why your name is on it."

And for the rest of my life, I've believed exactly what she told me. I'm special. Not because I'm better than others, but because I'm someone unique whom God created and am special in His eyes. I'm different. I stand out. It gave me a tremendous sense of identity. I understood who I was, where I came from, and what my family expected of me.

From an early age, I knew I was a descendant of Caribbean West Indian laborers who helped build the Panama Canal, the man-made waterway connecting the Atlantic and Pacific Oceans through the narrow Isthmus of Panama. It is one of the world's greatest engineering feats. History books often call it the "eighth wonder of the world."

Yet just as the federal government exploited the thousands of African-American farmers I represented in the largest civil rights settlement in U.S. history, they had also exploited the Black laborers who were so crucial to the construction of the Panama Canal. For more than a decade, Caribbean West Indian workers from countries such as Barbados, Guadeloupe, Martinique, and Trinidad dug, blasted, and hauled away more than 268 million cubic yards of earth—enough to bury Manhattan to a depth of 12 feet.[4] My ancestors were among those workers.

Before the Panama Canal was completed, ships sailing between the East and West Coasts of the U.S. had to navigate their way around treacherous Cape Horn, located off the shore of southern Chile. The Cape's waters are especially hazardous because of powerful gales, large whitecaps, strong currents, and, depending upon the season, daunting icebergs. It was why ship captains from long ago warned their crews, "Below 40 degrees latitude, there is no law; below 50, there is no God."

Legend has it that the English explorer Sir Francis Drake took one look at Cape Horn and turned farther south. Spanish conquistadors were so frightened of its dark, haunted waters that they transported their looted Aztec and Mayan gold across land. Yet for nearly three centuries, Cape Horn was the only nautical passage for ships sailing from the Atlantic to the Pacific.

In 1869, the French completed construction of the Suez Canal in Egypt, connecting the Mediterranean and Red Seas. Soon thereafter, they were inspired to try to build the Panama Canal as well. While the Panama Canal would be only 40 percent as long as the Suez Canal, the French were grossly unprepared for the tropical climate, rainy season, and the dangers hiding in Panama's dense rainforests, including venomous snakes and spiders.

Even worse were the outbreaks of deadly mosquito-borne illnesses such as malaria and yellow fever. It is estimated that 22,000 workers died during the attempted French construction, but the toll was likely higher than that.[5] As one of several books on this architectural feat points out, "…the truth was partly suppressed or minimized by the Canal Company in order not to destroy the confidence of the people in the project, and outside of the hospital rolls, the records were incomplete."[6] The authors added, "A virulent form of malaria, known as 'Chagres fever,' caused a greater toll in lives than any other one disease. The negro laborers, although immune from yellow fever, succumbed quickly to attacks of this form of malaria."[7]

Finally in 1889, after spending more than $287 million and squandering the savings of more than 800,000 investors, the French effort to build a sea-level canal ended in bankruptcy.[8] In June 1902, the U.S. Senate passed the Spooner Act, which authorized purchasing the French assets remaining in Panama, presuming the U.S. would successfully negotiate a treaty with Columbia, which controlled Panama at the time.

When the countries couldn't reach such a deal, President Theodore Roosevelt supported Panamanian rebels fighting for their freedom and in November 1903 recognized the new independent government that emerged. The U.S. and Panama quickly signed the Hay-Bunau-Varilla Treaty, which gave America the rights to build and indefinitely manage the Panama Canal Zone. The U.S. paid France $40 million for their holdings that remained there, including excavation equipment and a railroad.

The Isthmian Canal Commission ultimately decided that a lock-and-lake canal system was the most feasible to construct. The commission "started by working aggressively to discipline the landscape and its inhabitants. They drained swamps, killed mosquitoes and initiated a whole-scale sanitation project. A new police force, schools and hospitals would also bring the region to what English geographer Vaughan Cornish celebrated as 'marvelous respectability.'"[9]

In truth, the destruction that took place to make way for this effort was devastating. "Whole villages and forests were flooded, and a railway constructed in the 1850s had to be relocated. The greatest challenge of all was the Culebra Cut, now known as the Gaillard Cut, an artificial valley excavated through some 13 kilometres of mountainous terrain. More than 100 million cubic metres of dirt had to be moved; the work consumed more than eight million kilograms of dynamite in three years alone."[10]

More than anything else, the commission needed labor. After the deaths of so many French workers to yellow fever and malaria, White Americans were reluctant to expose themselves to the horrid tropical conditions and grave dangers of blasting rock. As a result, tens of thousands of contract workers, mostly Blacks from the Caribbean, built the Panama Canal.

By the end of 1912, there were an estimated 30,619 laborers from the West Indies working toward this goal, including 19,444 from Barbados; 5,542 from Martinique; 2,053 from Guadeloupe; and 1,427 from Trinidad.[11] Promises of lucrative employment and wealth lured them there, but they confronted an entirely different reality. "To them, the Culebra Cut was 'Hell's Gorge.' They lived like second-class citizens, subject to a Jim Crow-like regime, with bad food, long hours and low pay. And constant danger."[12]

According to hospital records and data from the Panama Canal Authority, diseases and accidents killed 5,609 workers during the American-led project. The fatalities included 4,500 Caribbean West Indian workers. By contrast, a reported 350 White Americans were killed.[13] Hundreds, if not thousands, of West Indian workers were permanently injured, including the loss of limbs from botched blasts and falling rocks.

My maternal great-grandfather, Samuel Augustus Jordan, and maternal great-grandmother, Kathryn Louisa Green, were among the many Black islanders who left their homes and jobs at sugar cane plantations to work on the canal. My great-grandfather was born in Cuba and raised in Barbados. My great-grandmother was born in Speightstown, Barbados. They met while working at the canal and married sometime later. They had two children; my great-aunt Sybil was born in 1910 and my grandmother in 1924.

About 10 percent of Barbados's total population and 40 percent of its men worked on the canal, earning and saving money to send home to relatives.[14] Barbados, the most easterly of the Caribbean islands, has a population of about 287,000 today. It is estimated that about 16 percent of Panama's 3.7 million population traces its roots directly back to Caribbean nations, including Barbados and Cuba.[15] My family members are included in that count.

In so many ways, the Panama Canal Zone, which covered 553 square miles along the canal and was controlled by the U.S. until 1979, was like an American Southern town that had been transplanted to Central America. If that conjures up pleasant images for you, you should know that it had its challenges as well. "It wasn't all idyllic—for a long time, the zone was segregated between American and Caribbean workers, with everything from shops to latrines designated as 'gold' (for Americans) and 'silver' (for West Indian and Caribbean workers). During construction on the earlier Panama Railroad in the middle of the 19th Century, Americans were paid higher wages in gold and West Indians received lower salaries in silver. School desegregation and the enforcement of the Civil Rights Act did not come until the 1970s, almost 20 years after being implemented in the US."[16]

For "Zonians" living on the "gold roll," life was good. Movie theaters screened the latest films from Hollywood, commissaries were stacked with familiar foods and other necessities from back home, and restaurants served cheeseburgers, French fries, Coca-Colas, and milkshakes. Outside of the zone, however, many Panamanians lived in extreme poverty—and so did many of the West Indian laborers and their families. The Panama Canal offered little to no economic benefit for the people who had lived there before its construction. Panamanians weren't hired to work at the locks, build housing, or service ships passing through.

As hostilities between the U.S. and Panama heightened during the 1950s, Americans erected a wall between the sovereign Canal Zone and Panama City. In 1964, tensions reached a boiling point when a group of students from the Instituto Nacional marched into the Canal Zone and demanded that the Panamanian flag be flown above Balboa High School. When staff refused to do so, the students rioted and destroyed property. American forces responded with tear gas. The riots left twenty-eight people dead, many of them Panamanians. Today, January 9 is still commemorated in Panama as "Martyrs' Day."[17]

I was born in Panama City on May 2, 1968, four years after the student-led uprising. My mother, Annette Burgess, was the oldest of Grandma Muriel's ten children. She was 26 years of age when I came along; my father, Enoes Francis, was several years older than she. My mother was living at home with her parents then, so I was one more kid among her many siblings. My uncle, who is five years older than me, was more like a brother.

On the day I was born, my father wasn't at the hospital. He worked as a firefighter with rotating twenty-four-hour shifts. Shortly after I came into the world, my mother's cousin, who was there with my mother, went to a pay phone and called my dad.

"Hey, you have a son," she told him.

To celebrate his first child's birth, my father went downstairs and found the runner for a local bookie who operated the daily numbers lottery. He bought as many "02" tickets as he could afford since I was born on the second day of May.

Well, as luck would have it, those numbers hit that night, and my dad won so much money—about thirty thousand dollars—that the bookie had to pay him in installments. Obviously that was quite a bit of change in 1968. Ever since my mother shared that story with me a few years ago, I like to tell my friends and colleagues, "Always bet on Greg. It's your best chance to win."

The area I grew up in is where many "Canal Zone brats" lived over the years. The French started digging there in 1888 and by the time the Americans took over, there were only nine usable buildings remaining.

To understand how the Panama Canal works, you first have to understand that the Pacific Ocean sits a bit higher than the Atlantic Ocean. The canal is about fifty miles in length from deep water in the Atlantic to deep water in the Pacific. "This difference in the sea level requires ships to get up over the terrain of Panama—up to 26 meters above the sea level—in order to reach the other end of the canal. With the help of Lock Gates, the vessels entering the canal are lifted to the higher level and later dropped down to the sea level at the other end of the canal."[18]

In other words, the locks work like a massive escalator, using water from a man-made lake to raise and then lower ships across the Continental Divide from the Atlantic Ocean to the Pacific Ocean, and vice versa. On average, it takes ships about eight hours to cross the canal. It saves crews about 7,900 miles by not having to sail around South America's southern tip.[19] My great-grandfather, Samuel Augustus Jordan, whom I mentioned earlier, was in charge of a crew of mules, which are actually tow train locomotives that help steer large ships through the canal, preventing them from hitting and damaging the canal. My grandfather, Claude Burgess, was a timekeeper, making sure the intricate system worked efficiently.

My neighborhood of Pedro Miguel is in the middle of the locks, where the canal's descent back to sea level begins. Following construction of the Pedro Miguel Locks in 1913, about sixty-two Americans and 162 alien workers and their families were selected to remain there to operate the system.[20] The U.S. government built new housing, police and fire stations, a restaurant, post office, barber shop, and clubhouse.

My mother's family moved there from Paraíso, a Canal Zone town to the north.

During the first four years of my life, when my mother and I lived with my maternal grandparents, we were housed in a duplex built by the U.S. government. It was a square, cookie-cutter home that looked like all of the others on our street. It was constructed from cinder blocks that were painted white, and it had a carport. There were three bedrooms in our unit, and I slept with my mother for the first few years. While my grandfather worked at the locks, my mother did clerical work at the Navy Exchange commissary.

On most days, I stood outside in our yard during the late afternoon hours, waiting for my grandfather to return home from work. My grandfather was a slim, good-looking man. He had a regal gait about him, and I could see him cresting the hill above our house. Part of his job was unloading cargo from ships, where he would find newspapers and magazines from far-away lands. He folded them into hats for me. I couldn't wait to get those hats every day.

As an adult, I've often wondered what was so special about them. Was it simply that he made them for me? About five years ago, it finally hit me. Sure, the hats were sentimental because my grandfather made them with his hands—and only for me. But what truly made them treasures was what happened once I unfolded the hats. Those newspapers and magazines opened an entirely different world to me.

I saw photographs of places that were thousands of miles away from the Panama Canal Zone. Ships from all over the world passed through the canal each day. I was too young to be reading yet, but those photographs jumped off the pages at me. For the first time in my life, I saw pictures of landmarks in the U.S., England, Russia, China, Japan, Australia, and everywhere in between. I saw Big Ben, the Great Wall of China, the Empire State Building, Mount Fuji, and the Great Barrier Reef. Sure, I was living near a great landmark myself—one my own forefathers toiled to build and operate—but these images gave me an entirely different idea of what my life could be and how far I could go.

Another strong influence in my life is my faith. I grew up in a Christian home from a very early age. In Panama, we attended church two or three times a week, and that's not even including Sundays, when you would definitely find me sitting in a pew at St. Alban's Episcopal. My grandparents, especially my grandmother, instilled Biblical principles in me: design, authority, responsibility, suffering, ownership, freedom, and success.

Even though my grandfather was a kindhearted man, he had a very exacting standard. He expected and demanded that we do well in school and be obedient. I think that is why his children were so successful. Each of them graduated in the top 20 percent of his or her class. Some were in the military, others became dentists and airline workers. Eventually my grandparents left Panama and moved to New Orleans, where my grandfather worked as a houseman at Xavier University. His job allowed one of my uncles to go to college for free.

Of course, my parents shaped my identity in intentional and unintentional ways too. My mother and father were never married. I'm not sure of the exact reasons but they never lived together after I was born. However, my father was still a very important part of my life as a child. Whenever he wasn't working at the fire station, he picked me up from school. He took me to get treats, brought me to his house so he could spend time with me, and we'd go to the park or beach together before he'd return me to my grandparents' home. Even though we didn't live together, I still loved my father very much.

While my mother was working at the Navy Exchange, she met a U.S. naval officer named John Thompson who was stationed in the Panama Canal Zone. John was from Columbia, South Carolina. He and my mother married on December 1, 1972. When John retired from the navy shortly thereafter, they decided to move to the U.S.

About a year later, on December 11, 1973, I boarded a plane with my mother and sister, after my stepfather went ahead of us. I was wearing a suit that my grandmother had made for me. Later that day, my father arrived to pick me up at school, but I wasn't there

Without warning, I was thrown into an entirely different world—one that would raise deeper questions about my identity, who I was, and where I came from.

CHAPTER TWO

———•———

NEW WORLD

TAP, TAP, TAP, TAP!

As I lay in my bed many nights after moving to the States, I struggled to fall asleep because of the constant clicking noise coming from the kitchen of my parents' home. My stepfather worked as a state correctional officer at a halfway house after retiring from the Navy. My mother was employed at a commissary on a nearby military base.

In order for my stepfather to earn a promotion and higher salary in the Florida Department of Corrections, he had to have a college degree. There was only one problem: he didn't like to write. So he recorded his lectures while taking classes at Valencia Community College in Orlando, Florida, and then my mother would transcribe the tapes for him late at night. For hours, she sat at the kitchen table, repeatedly hitting the play and pause buttons on an old-time cassette recorder as she typed away. To be honest, I wondered if the clicking noise would ever leave my head.

When we departed Panama in December 1973, I didn't know very much English. My mother's family mostly spoke Spanish at home before then. Before I started kindergarten at Pineloch Elementary School, my mother put very entertaining tutors in charge of teaching me English—Bert and Ernie, the Jetsons, Captain Kangaroo, and the Jeffersons. I'm not kidding; that's how I learned to speak English, with my mom and stepdad correcting me as I went along.

I must have sat in front of that TV for fourteen hours each day. My older sister, Pam, and I were the only kids in our neighborhood who spoke with an accent and "weren't from here." She had a more outgoing personality than I did and was able to make friends. I was sort of a recluse during those first few years in the U.S. In fact, my mom swears that one of our neighbors didn't even know she had a son until after we had lived in our house for four years. That's how much I stayed inside. Pam was my protector and was typically the one retaliating against bullies. We were best friends.

Once I mastered English, I didn't look back. In the first grade, the teachers wanted to promote me to the fourth grade because my reading and writing skills were so advanced. I had learned to write my name in cursive at the Panamanian preschool. My parents thought I was too young and small to make such a leap, so I was placed in a program for gifted kids. It was a new program in which kids from multiple schools were bused to another school for certain classes. There was one other Black child in my gifted class. I thought the other kids in the new school were different. I hid in the restroom when it came time for me to catch the bus to go there. Eventually, a teacher would escort me from my classroom to the bus to make sure I got on.

Faith, as I mentioned, has always been an important part of my life. I guess that comes from my grandparents. In the fourth grade, I read my Bible from cover to cover. I liked to read books, build model cars, and watch TV. I especially liked going to church because it reminded me of Panama. I was happy one of my mother's co-workers introduced us to St. John's Baptist Church in Tangerine, Florida, where we joined the congregation shortly after moving to the U.S.

Of course, there were plenty of chores for my sister and I to do around the house. As you might guess, my stepfather, a thirty-year Navy chief petty officer, ran a very tight ship. Each morning, I had to make my bed well enough to pass inspection. I still make my bed every morning, even today. As retired Admiral William H. McRaven wrote in his book *Make Your Bed*, our daily lives need structure. "Nothing can replace the strength and comfort of one's faith, but sometimes the simple act of making your bed can give you the lift you need to start your day and provide you the satisfaction to end it right."[21]

Along with making my bed, I was required to line my shoes up in the closet, and everything else in my bedroom had to be orderly. There was no roughhousing or arguing with my sister. I rarely spoke back to my mom or stepdad. He demanded respect and discipline in everything I did. I guess when you spend your days around inmates and convicts, you want to be sure that your stepson will never end up like them. My stepfather was a wonderful provider and worked very hard. We didn't have the traditional father-son relationship. He wasn't very affectionate, nor did he interact very much with me, other than when it was time for disciplining me.

Even though I was adjusting well academically and socially in Orlando, I still felt like there was something missing in my life. I didn't understand why my parents had uprooted me from my home in Panama, or why they separated me from the father, grandparents, aunts, uncles, and cousins who loved me. Most of all, I didn't know why they dumped me in the middle of a new country where I knew no one else but my sister and them. It was a mystery that confounded me for much of my early life.

Moreover, it wasn't until I was a teenager that I had an inkling of this event's impact on my birth father. I discovered that after I left, he showed up at school that day to pick me up as usual. When the teachers told him I wasn't there, he went to my grandparents' home to look for me. That's when my grandmother told him that I wasn't returning. She explained that I had left for the U.S. with my mom and sister.

He had a trunkful of Christmas presents for me that day.

For whatever reason (I didn't muster the courage to ask my mom about it all until much later in life), I didn't have contact with my father for the next several years. Growing up, I could only assume that he didn't want me because he never came to find me. My dad ultimately remarried and according to my younger sister, Kathia Dennis, he didn't talk about me very much. However, each year on my birthday she told me that he became very depressed and quiet.

Even looking back now, I can't imagine the emotional pain he suffered when I left. I'm sure it was especially hurtful because he had grown up in similar circumstances. According to my relatives, my dad was born out of wedlock and didn't know his father until he was an adult. In fact, he believed his name was Leonard Fisher until he realized later in life it was actually Enoes Francis.

Inexplicably, my dad's mother never told his father that he had a son. My dad lived with his mother until he was about six years old. Then, on April 18, 1940, they lost their apartment in a massive fire in Colon, Panama. The windswept blaze was sixteen blocks wide and left about ten thousand people homeless. The fire happened on the Atlantic side of the Panama Canal. It was so bad that firefighters had to dynamite buildings to help contain its spread. After losing her home, my grandmother sent my father to live with her older sister, whose house hadn't been damaged. My paternal grandmother was among the thousands of canal workers and other Panamanians who were forced to live in tents until Colon was rebuilt.

I didn't learn those details about my father's life until I was an adult. As a child, I only had a fading memory of my dad, and a burning desire to see him again.

Apparently, my father reached out to my mom's sister and her husband at some point about helping him make contact with me. When they called my mother, however, his request wasn't well received. As Kathia grew up, she wanted to have a relationship with her older brother. So her mother called my mom, and a meeting in Orlando was finally planned.

In 1982, when I was around fourteen years old, my younger sister flew to Orlando with her mom and my dad to visit Walt Disney World®

Resort and to see me. My mother arranged for me to meet them at their hotel, and we had a great day together. They brought me back that evening, and my stepfather was already home from work. Apparently, my mother hadn't told him about me seeing my dad. Well, John threw my father, sister, and my sister's mother out of our house. That was the last time I would see my dad for nearly fourteen years.

After so many years apart, Kathia reached out to me on her own, sending a letter shortly after I graduated from law school. She reintroduced herself and told me that she and my father loved me. At the time, I was so angry with my dad. I didn't understand why he never made contact or never fought to have a relationship with me in those intervening years. Having kids of my own now, I'm convinced that nothing or no one could possibly keep me away from my children.

Kathia later told me that she very much wanted to see me over the years but my dad was reluctant to try again because of what had happened in Orlando. I'm certain he was only protecting himself after having his heart broken. In fact, that's what ended up killing him—a broken heart. He had suffered from rheumatic fever as a boy, which severely weakened his heart as an adult. In 1979, he had heart surgery and lived another twenty years. He followed Kathia and her mother to New York when they moved there in 1987. My dad was a building inspector in New York until he was too sick to work anymore. He suffered at least two heart attacks.

By the time Kathia and I had reconnected, I was working as a defense attorney, and I occasionally prepared and interviewed expert witnesses in New York. During those trips, Kathia and I would have dinner together. Because of my anger toward my dad, I never invited him to join us. Finally, Kathia took the bull by the horns. After she picked me up from my hotel during one of those visits, she informed me that we weren't going to eat.

"We're going to see Daddy," she said.

She hadn't even told him that I was coming. When I walked into his apartment, he was sitting on the couch. He looked up and didn't say a word. I couldn't speak either. We probably hugged and cried for ten minutes. He had recently suffered a stroke and undergone open-heart surgery so he couldn't speak much anyway. I'm not sure there was anything that needed to be said. All of the bitterness and anger that I had felt for so long was suddenly gone. My belief that he had never wanted me vanished. I knew the man loved me and had missed me dearly.

I probably visited with my father three or more times over the next year. We talked on the phone every now and then, and I felt I had plenty of time to get to know him since we had reconnected. He died of heart failure in March 1999. After his death, my stepmother, Jeannette Francis, assured me that my dad loved me like nothing and like no one else in the world. Before they were married, he made her promise that they would never have children because he couldn't go through the emotional toll of possibly losing one again. He was quite upset when she became pregnant with Kathia. Of course, he was a great father to her and loved her as much as he did me.

———•—•———

When I was younger, I played football and ran track at Oak Ridge High School in Orlando. As a junior and senior, I had a job at McDonald's, the one right next to SeaWorld. I saved enough money to buy my first car—a yellow Ford Pinto. It was the coolest car on my street. Then again, I think I was one of the few kids in my neighborhood who owned a car. I spent most days working out with my best friends, Tony Glover, Reggie Demps, and Kevin Walker, with whom I am still close today. We played football together and were inseparable.

While I was in high school, my mother operated a daycare out of our house to help save money for me to attend college. I applied to only one school, the University of Florida, because it was close to home, that's where everyone in my senior class was trying to go, and I could afford the in-state tuition. I was naive to the entire college process, and I didn't want to have to pay another fifteen-dollar application fee at another school. When Florida accepted me in the spring of 1986, I decided I was going to be a Gator.

Since I had excelled in math and science classes in high school, I was set on becoming an aerospace engineer. I wanted to be a "rocket scientist" and work for NASA. A few of my friends who were also going to Florida attended a summer program to prove their academic worth. Not me. I was the smart one in the gifted classes, or so I thought.

I figured my studies would be just as manageable as before, so I overloaded my schedule during my first semester of college. The course catalog suggested that I take calculus, chemistry, English, and an elective right off the bat, and that's what I did. Never mind dipping your toes in the water; I jumped right into the deep end of higher education. Well, I quickly realized I had bitten off more than I could chew. At the end of that semester I had a 1.5 grade-point average. I flunked calculus, had a D in chemistry, a C+ in psychology, and a B+ in English.

Near the end of the holiday break, my grades arrived at my parents' home and my mom opened them. Within minutes, she was packing my bags and sending me back to campus. I knew my mother was so disappointed in me. One of her favorite sayings was, "If better is possible, good isn't good enough." She must have thought I hadn't even tried to do well.

"If your stepfather sees these grades, you won't be going back to school," she told me. "You'll be going into the military."

John never understood why I hadn't joined the Navy and let the federal government pay for my education. If nothing else, my grades showed me that I probably didn't have the right stuff to be an engineer. Since I had made a decent grade in the English class, the professor encouraged me to pursue a degree that involved writing. That spring, my grades turned around with hard work, and I had done well enough to return as a sophomore.

During my second semester at Florida, I met an older engineering student, Cedric Washington, who invited me to attend study sessions at the library with his brothers from Kappa Alpha Psi fraternity. I joined that fraternity, and those guys became my best friends and supporters. With their help and encouragement, I became a very good student. In fact, I was invited to join Florida's oldest and most prestigious leadership honorary society, the Florida Blue Key. Its past members include governors, U.S. senators, *The Washington Post* publisher Phil Graham, and Heisman Trophy winners Steve Spurrier and Tim Tebow. When I was invited to join, there were two hundred active members, and I was one of only three Black students. I also joined the Savant Leadership Honorary group and served as the Honor Court's chancellor.

When I graduated from Florida in 1991 with a Bachelor of Arts in Criminal Justice, I had a 3.5 grade-point average. A few of my fraternity brothers who were also criminal justice majors planned to become police officers or correctional officers. After growing up with John and hearing about his interactions with inmates, the idea of working in law enforcement wasn't at all appealing to me.

At 23 years old, I wasn't sure what I wanted to do with the rest of my life. To be honest, I only knew that I wasn't ready to leave Gainesville. Spurrier had just returned as the Gators' football coach, and I was having a great time going to school there. One of my fraternity brothers, Willie Jackson, was a wide receiver on the team, and my best friend and roommate, Renaldo Garcia, was a Gators basketball player.

The idea of attending law school was in the back of my mind. Having grown up in a neighborhood in which you had to make potentially life-altering decisions every day, I was fortunate that my stepfather was as strict as he was. He and my mother kept me on the straight and narrow path.

Others weren't so fortunate. One of my close friends, Frank Scott, who grew up with me in Richmond Heights, was one of those guys who ruined his life because of poor decisions. In March 1991, when Frank was 23 years old, he was arrested for murdering a 26-year-old woman in an Orlando hotel room. During a visit I had with him in prison, he told me it was unintentional and a mistake. He burglarized a home and committed assault before police arrested him. Frank was sentenced to life in prison in April 1992. Even to this day, it isn't lost on me that as I was starting my quest to become a lawyer, Frank was facing the prospect of spending the rest of his life in prison.

Frank wasn't the only kid in my neighborhood who threw his life away. The consequences of those choices left an indelible mark on me. While some of the people I knew made terrible decisions and deserved punishment, others made youthful mistakes that were blown out of proportion. Yet they were categorized as criminals and thugs and were trapped by those labels. The area in which I grew up was sort of a proving ground where I saw both justice and injustice play out over and over again on the ball courts, playgrounds, and streets. I was determined to stay on a path that would one day put me in a position to make a real difference.

One afternoon, I was walking by the campus bookstore and boldly decided that I would try to attend the University of Florida Fredric G. Levin College of Law. I knew my parents couldn't afford to pay for an LSAT prep course, nor were they going to be supportive of me continuing my time in Gainesville as I was already in my fifth year, so I purchased a prep book instead. I found the date of the next LSAT test being offered. It was forty days away so I divided the number of pages in the book by forty and went to work. I ended up doing well enough on the exam to be admitted.

Everything about law school was so foreign to me. I was anxious about the entire process. I hadn't been that interested in law before. It was never a topic of discussion in our home. I didn't know any African-American lawyers in Orlando, and there weren't many Black students attending law school back then either. Everything was so new and unique to me. As a result of my grade-point average, student activities, and LSAT score, I was awarded a Virgil Hawkins Fellowship. With the assistance of patient professors and helpful mentors, I grew more comfortable with the coursework and what would be expected of me. I made the Dean's List and received writing and oral honors in appellate advocacy. I was even appointed as a Justice for the University of Florida Board of Masters, the highest Appellate Court for student disciplinary matters, and rose to the level of Senior Presiding Justice in 1994.

I was on my way to becoming an attorney. However, there was one big obstacle: many majority firms were not hiring minority clerks at the time. Most of those coveted positions were going to well-connected White students. After I struggled to land a summer clerkship, I volunteered in the law school's career services office. I learned how to build a resume and made connections with lawyers who contacted the office to hire clerks. Finally, I was hired as a summer clerk at the Bobo, Spicer, Fulford, et al defense firm in West Palm Beach, Florida.

This was the same law firm where I would end up starting my career after I completed my Juris Doctorate in 1994 from UF Law. At the time, I could never have imagined where this career would take me—or how I would become a voice for thousands of Blacks who hadn't had a voice for decades.

CHAPTER THREE

———◆———

DISCOVERING THE LAW

ELIEVE IT OR NOT, ONE OF THE REASONS I WAS ABLE TO SECURE A clerkship at one of the top medical malpractice law firms in the country was because I operated a monorail at Walt Disney World during the summers while attending the University of Florida. I'm serious.

Before I interviewed with the senior associates who would be responsible for the clerkship program at Bobo, Spicer, Fulford, et al, they had decided that they weren't going to hire the candidate with the best grades or even one who made law review. Instead, they were looking for a regular guy they could drink beer with. As luck would have it, a recent *Simpsons* episode they thought was especially funny had featured a monorail. When they heard about my summer experience, I naturally landed the summer clerkship. It was also fated that Joe Osborne, the senior associate with whom I worked most closely and who hired me, would later become my partner in my firm now.

At the end of my clerkship, the other partners asked Joe if I was qualified to be hired as an associate once I graduated. He said I was, so I had a job lined up even before finishing law school. I just had to pass the bar. I moved to West Palm Beach and spent three months working in the firm's main office. When an associate at the firm's location in Orlando left for another job, they moved me there. Orlando was my hometown after all. I wasn't thrilled about moving back, but it was a tremendous opportunity for a recent law school graduate. Since it was a small satellite office, I was able to argue motions in the courtroom and handle depositions. It was a great experience. I spent the next seven years, including the last three as a partner, representing doctors, hospitals, and other defendants in medical malpractice cases.

In 2000 I opposed H. Scott Bates in a malpractice case. Scott was an equity partner at Morgan Colling & Gilbert and the right-hand man to the firm's founder, John Morgan. He must have liked my work because he called me a few weeks later and asked if I'd be interested in joining their practice. At the time, Morgan's firm hadn't achieved its status yet as the state's largest plaintiffs' personal injury firm. You may be familiar with them from their TV commercials and their billboards on interstate highways, featuring the slogan "For the People." Today Morgan & Morgan is huge, with more than seven hundred attorneys and offices all over the country. Its website claims the firm has recovered $9 billion for its clients thus far. But back then, they had about forty-five attorneys concentrated in their Orlando and Tampa offices.

My life was changing in other ways too. From a very young age, I knew I was going to get married and start a family. I wanted to be a father. The first time I met my wife, Keisha, she was attending Bethune-Cookman University, a historically Black college in Daytona Beach, Florida. She grew up there because her father, Samuel Berry, had been hired as the marching band director in 1969. He directed the famed Marching Wildcats for the next ten years and laid the groundwork for the success they have today. If you've ever been to an HBCU football game, you might already know the band's halftime shows are just as important as the game itself. Keisha's father passed away in 1980. He was inducted into the Bethune-Cookman University athletics hall of fame posthumously in 2012 for his tremendous leadership and vision.

Keisha and I met when I was still attending the University of Florida. Two of my fraternity brothers had girlfriends attending Bethune-Cookman, and they were constantly trying to introduce me to one of their friends. The first time I visited the school, it just wasn't my cup of tea. My fraternity brothers kept telling me how pretty Keisha was, and I told them I thought I was doing okay at UF when it came to romance. I just wasn't that interested. The following spring break, I was in Daytona for the weekend and went to a party. Keisha was there as well. "There she is. There she is," they said.

Well, she was quite attractive, so I asked her to dance. We talked briefly afterward and then parted ways. When we were on the beach the next day, Keisha walked by again. I called her name, and she looked me up and down as if she had no idea who I was. Everyone started to laugh. "This is why I don't like Daytona Beach," I said.

My older fraternity brothers ended up marrying those girlfriends and lived in Daytona so I would drive down to see them from time to time. They would invite Keisha for dinner and to hang out, and soon she and I became very good friends. We ended up dating for six or seven months after I graduated from law school. She was working in pharmaceutical sales in Miami, but she would fly to Orlando and stay with me, then drive over to Daytona Beach to see her mom. She's an only child so those visits were important to both of them. We ended up breaking things off because she was busy living her life in Miami and I was busy living mine in Orlando. I continued to date other girls. But it was my stepfather, John Thompson, who made me realize what a mistake I had made.

"Why are you dating all these other girls when you should be with that one?" he asked me.

In January 1999, Super Bowl XXXIII was held in Miami Gardens, Florida. I flew down to attend the game with a friend. However, that afternoon, I called Keisha and invited her to lunch. She picked out the restaurant and I arrived early to get us a table. She walked in and wasn't wearing anything special—a white button-down shirt over blue jeans and heels. But as soon as I saw her, it was suddenly clear as day to me. I thought to myself, *That's what your wife is supposed to look like.*

She was dating someone else at the time and I was too. Shortly thereafter we decided to start seeing each other again and were engaged by Christmas Day later that year. We were married at Daytona Beach on September 30, 2000. Our daughter, Grier, was born in 2003, and our son, Gregorio (we call him Rio), came along three years later. Keisha was a very successful pharmaceutical saleswoman. She decided to stay home with the kids in 2010, and she's a wonderful mother and wife.

By that point in my career, I had represented dozens of clients and tried nine medical malpractice cases, which were quite a few given the number of years I had been practicing. My career seemed to be on the path that I had envisioned in law school. I was on the typical ascent of a defense attorney. I had never considered becoming a personal injury attorney and really hadn't learned much about that area of law in college. But after Scott called me a couple of times, I agreed to an interview.

I would soon learn that I had quite a bit in common with John Morgan, who offered me a job after my interview in 2001. We both came from meager beginnings. John grew up in a poor Catholic family in Louisville, Kentucky, before moving to central Florida in 1971. When he was a sophomore at the University of Florida in 1976, his younger brother, Tim, was injured while working as a lifeguard at Walt Disney World.[22] He was paralyzed from the chest down in the accident, which is one of the reasons John pursued a career in personal injury law. In many ways, John is an overachiever like me. He was also a member of Florida Blue Key and thrived at UF. He is a great communicator and uses it to his advantage.

After spending the first seven years of my law career as a defense attorney, I switched sides and represented plaintiffs at Morgan Colling & Gilbert. I was assigned to the personal injury section where I had a steep learning curve at first. I didn't have trouble signing up clients, but I probably wasn't clearing out cases as quickly as they wanted in such a fast-paced environment. I moved to the medical malpractice side and represented parents whose babies had suffered brain damage during deliveries because of negligent circumstances, people who had suffered spinal cord injuries and were paralyzed, and others who had catastrophic injuries from auto wrecks. I was quite successful helping my clients get justice there.

In early 2005, two of the co-founders of the firm, Stewart L. Colling and Ron Gilbert, decided to leave to start their own firm. John was our frontman, and Stewart and Ron did great work in the courtroom and behind the scenes. At the time, John said it was an amicable split over a fundamental difference about growth. "They wanted to go slower, simpler, and safer," John told the *Orlando Sentinel* in February 2005. "My pace is more like a MiG fighter jet. That's what drove Stewart and Ron crazy. I would keep opening offices in other cities."[23]

John's vision has always been to grow or die. He felt that if we weren't moving into new practice areas, hiring additional attorneys, or opening new offices, we weren't thriving. Within six months of joining the firm, we launched two new locations in Florida, first in Naples and then in Jacksonville. By the time of the breakup, we had opened offices in Arizona and New York as well. John's next move was to ask a group of lawyers he thought were valuable to the firm to become shareholders. There were five such lawyers who accepted this offer and became shareholders in Morgan Law Firm PA. I was among them.

While that might sound like a tremendous opportunity for a 37-year-old attorney, it also required those of us who said yes to borrow substantial amounts of money in order to participate. The way the arrangement worked was for individual shareholders to purchase interest in individual offices. Because the firm was investing so rapidly in expansion, it was likely to be a while before these new ventures would be profitable for us. Although there was never a question about the firm surviving, it did take a couple of years for us to see a nice return on our investments. Before long, I had financial interests in our Atlanta, Nashville, and Jackson, Mississippi offices, as well as in the Orlando office where I made my original investment.

By late 2007, I was spending quite a bit of time in Mississippi investigating whether or not our firm should become involved in the "donning and doffing class action cases." In 2002, Perdue Farms Inc. reached an agreement with the U.S. Department of Labor in which the poultry producer agreed to change its pay practices to compensate workers for the time they spent donning (putting on) and doffing (taking off) the personal protective equipment they needed to wear to perform their jobs.

The U.S. Supreme Court later sided with workers at a slaughter and meat processing plant in Washington and a poultry processing plant in Maine, determining that they must be considered on the clock when they're in the process of donning and doffing their PPE. There were quite a few poultry processing plants in Mississippi, and I wanted to know if these practices were occurring there as well. While it might take only ten or fifteen minutes to put on and take off PPE, that time adds up to quite a lot of money over a few years. After the high court ruling, the class-action lawsuits expanded to include hotel workers, oilmen, auto workers, police officers, fire fighters, and just about every other occupation that required employees to wear PPE.

When I went to Mississippi, I brought along my confidant and close childhood friend Tony Glover and a recent hire by me, Carlos Leach. Tony and I had remained friends throughout adulthood and because of his large frame, I had hired him as my protector and primary investigator. Carlos was one of our firm's young associates and a native of the Magnolia State. Carlos grew up in Jackson and was an All-American kicker at Southern University in Baton Rouge, Louisiana. His mother was the twin sister of former U.S. Secretary of Agriculture Mike Espy. We shared office space with Mike and he eventually joined our firm in a joint venture involving the donning and doffing cases. In 2009, our firm helped recover more than $1 million for workers at Wayne Farms plants, who hadn't been paid for time spent walking to the production line and donning and doffing their PPE.

During one of our meetings, Mike mentioned in passing that there might be additional cases in the *Pigford v. Glickman* class-action lawsuit that involved Black farmers. I'll be honest: I didn't know much about the case at the time and wasn't too interested. It wouldn't be very long, however, before I was knee-deep in what would become the largest civil rights class-action lawsuit in U.S. history.

CHAPTER FOUR

———•———

CHAMPIONING THE CAUSE

P IGFORD V. GLICKMAN, THE FIRST OF TWO RELATED CLASS-ACTION
lawsuits at the center of this book, began on August 28, 1997, when a
Black farmer named Timothy Pigford and 400 other plaintiffs filed
a federal suit against the USDA and then-Secretary of Agriculture Dan
Glickman. The plaintiffs alleged racial discrimination against African-
Americans in the agency's allocations of farm loans and assistance
between 1983 and 1997. Although the lawsuit was specific to actions that
took place during the 1980s and 1990s, the plaintiffs claimed that the
USDA, "a racist plantation, disguised as a government agency—had
discriminated against Black farmers and it had done so since the Civil
War." These farmers wanted compensatory damages—money. They also
wanted injunctive relief, which would provide the legal assurance that
no Black farmers after them would receive anything less than equal, fair,
and full treatment.

The case garnered the support of pioneers in the political and legal realms who fought for the full rights of Black people to vote—pioneers who had also battled election fraud and voter suppression, helped desegregate schools, and championed civil rights cases during other key moments and movements in American history. One of those figures was J. L. Chestnut Jr., who in 1958 became the first Black lawyer in his hometown of Selma, Alabama, and who was an attorney for the Rev. Dr. Martin Luther King Jr. and his aides and demonstrators.

J. L. was born on December 16, 1930, to a mother who was a school-teacher and a father who owned a grocery store. He graduated with a degree in business administration from Dillard University in New Orleans in 1953, then served two years in the Army before earning his law degree in 1958 from Howard University in Washington, D.C.

He was a man who witnessed one of the most transformational events in our nation's history and was a confidant of people who helped change its course. He stood up for MLK Jr. and John Lewis in the 1960s. He never forgot that Bloody Sunday in Selma on March 7, 1965. Chestnut was on the phone with the NAACP when he saw Lewis and marchers at the Edmund Pettus Bridge go face-to-face with the police.[24]

"And then John and the others began to kneel and pray," he told NPR in 1990. "And then I heard something that sounded like a tear gas canister hit the pavement. And then there was smoke, bedlam, confusion, blood, tears, cries. And there were these big, hefty posse men swinging billy clubs the size of baseball bats and coming down across the heads of women and children. My eyes were hurting, and my head was hurting, and New York was screaming over the telephone, What's going on? What's going on? And I tried to pull some women back out of the street, and it was just awful."[25]

That was a dark day for J.L. He said he "lost all faith in America" at that point, but two days later his faith was renewed when he saw Blacks and Whites rally and come together to continue the fight for change and voting rights. ". . . I saw hundreds and hundreds of people come from all over this land to join with us in this little town of my birth," he said. "And I had to look and reassess all over again. And my faith in this nation, my faith in the human race was restored."[26]

He was still fighting for Blacks, not just in Selma, but everywhere, when his firm, among others, filed the Pigford case.

He recognized that the *Pigford v. Glickman* was as much about civil rights as it was about farming. And although he didn't know much about agriculture, he later told farmers in Albany, Georgia, who were participating in the lawsuit, that for him it "...was as natural as putting on a raincoat when it begins to rain."[27]

One of J. L.'s partners in Chestnut, Sanders, Sanders and Pettaway LLC was Henry "Hank" Sanders. Hank was also present at the march in Selma and like J. L., he continued to take up the cause in innumerable ways throughout his life. He had been elected to the Alabama Senate in 1982 and served until 2018, the longest-serving state senator in Alabama.

In 1955, when Hank was just a teen, he and his twelve siblings lived in a three-room shack on a farm in Baldwin County, Alabama, just east of Mobile and on the Gulf Coast. His classmates at the time found it funny when he said he wanted to be an attorney. "I think they laughed at me because they had never seen a lawyer, especially one who was black," he recalled.[28] He went on to graduate from Harvard Law School before returning to Alabama to practice civil rights law.

Once in the late 1960s, Hank was waiting for his wife Rose at a Dairy Queen when a White man came up and pushed Rose out of the way. Hank got out of his car and asked, "What are you doing to my wife?" The guy yelled, "Get out of here," and then called him a racial slur. Hank told him, "You're not gonna do that to my wife." When he tried to grab the guy, the man took out a knife and stabbed Hank. The police came and let the guy go home while Hank was taken to jail with a stab wound. When his people came to bail him out, he refused. He said, "Bail is when you've done something. I will never acknowledge or admit that I had done something to him. He did something to me ...." You can't bail me out." The police ultimately released him.

This story speaks volumes about Hank's principles and self-respect. He brought these qualities to all the cases he fought, but he especially brought respect for Black farmers to the Pigford case. He not only recalled hearing MLK Jr. shouting, "How long?" and the crowd responding, "Not long!" on March 25, 1965,[29] he also recalled how, from

Selma to Montgomery, it was Black farmers who provided a place for folks who were marching to stop, spend the night, and even eat a meal.

About six years after the Selma march, in 1971, Hank returned to the Alabama city with his wife, Faya Ora Rose Toure (formerly Rose M. Sanders), to further pursue their legal careers and to help ensure full voting rights for Blacks (something he remained vocal about during the 2020 elections). The couple joined J. L. Chestnut's firm, and it was during that time that Hank also ran for state office, embarking on four decades of public service. By the time Chestnut, Sanders, Sanders and Pettaway LLC started working on the Pigford suit in the 1990s, it had grown to become the state's largest Black law firm and one of the largest in the U.S. It had thirteen attorneys and about thirty staffers.

There were many other direct life experiences that informed Hank's work on the Pigford case. He recalled growing up in southwestern Alabama on property that his family would not be able to own. It was clear to him then that Black farmers knew it was a waste of time to try to get a loan from the Farmers Home Administration. Either their loan requests would be denied, or if a loan was granted, the amount wasn't enough to cover their needs. In other instances, the sum granted arrived too late.

In the 1970s and 1980s, Hank and his wife did a lot of work with the Emergency Land Fund, which would later become part of the Federation of Southern Cooperatives. They focused on issues related to Black land loss, especially what happens when someone dies without a will. Both Hank and Rose fought tirelessly to ensure that the property in these instances was given by the state to the deceased person's heirs. The legal term for such land is "heir property."

"Land is such a powerful force in our lives and it means so much when you have land, so it's important to try to keep it," he explained years later. "But another thing that was brought forcefully to our attention was that much of the heir property was not being used. And that made it a lot easier to actually be lost."[30] He went on to say, "... we worked a lot on trying to get people to go ahead and put it into production. If it wasn't row crops, then put it into tree production—put it into some kind of production because then it was less likely to be lost."[31]

For Hank, the issue of heir property is a personal one. He frequently spoke about what his mother, Ola Mae Sanders, experienced as a way to demonstrate the importance of land loss among generations of Black families. It's one of the many powerful stories he's shared with me when we ultimately worked together. He lived on heir property growing up, but his father, Sam Sanders, wasn't the actual heir to the land because Hank's grandfather was still alive. Hank's mom worked for a White family, and when she would walk to and from her job, her employer's kids would taunt her on the road saying, "Look, you don't have any right to live on this land, you're not an heir. We're going to put you off."[32] They also said they would fire her when their daddy died. Hank described his mother as a fiery woman, but she accepted their jeers until she could no longer take it. She told her kids one summer that when they picked cotton in the fall, they weren't going to buy school clothes or books with the money they earned. She would take the money and purchase a piece of land. Hank remembered her saying, "I'm tired of them threatening me every morning and every evening."[33] When they had $50, she ". . . went to another county and put the $50 down on one acre of land that cost $150."[34] He believes the word got out. Nobody threatened her again. "We never lived on that land but it was an umbrella of freedom for her. That's the power of owning a piece of land. When you own land you look at yourself differently, but everyone else looks at you differently as well," he said later.[35]

Both Hank and J. L. understood the power of identity. They had developed it in themselves and they were cultivating it in Black farmers by encouraging them to stand up, be noticed, and demand what was rightfully theirs by virtue of inheritance and/or by virtue of the work they did and the value they continually brought to their communities through the food they provided. By contesting the USDA's unfair treatment of them when allocating price support loans, disaster loans, farm ownership loans, and operating loans, Black farmers were staking a claim in themselves as well as in their land.

After the case was filed, it was thought that 2,000 Black farmers were discriminated against by the USDA, not just the original 400 plaintiffs. At that point, the attorneys for Pigford requested what is called "blanket mediation" so as many Black farmers with claims could be accounted for in the dispute resolution. The U.S. Department of Justice opposed this, stating that each case needed to be investigated separately. As the case drew nearer, the presiding judge set some parameters by certifying the class in the suit to include all Black farmers who had filed discrimination complaints against the USDA between 1983 and 1997.

In 1999, Pigford was settled out of court, which in and of itself signaled quite an admission of wrongdoing on the part of the USDA.

Under the consent decree, a two-tiered mechanism for dispute resolution was established.

Under Track A, claimants who could successfully provide the basic evidence required by the DOJ and the USDA would receive $50,000, as well as relief in the form of loan forgiveness and offsets of tax liability.

Under Track B, claimants who could prove their claims and actual damages with a preponderance of evidence could have their documentation reviewed by a third-party arbitrator, who would then determine the relief amount in a binding decision. Based on the evidence, the relief could be more or less than the relief provided in Track A.

Claimants had 180 days from the consent decree to file.

As it happened, the number of farmers with disputes far exceeded earlier estimates. The claims of more than 22,000 Track A applications were heard and decided.

While Hank Sanders said at the time that Pigford was a "great victory,"[36] he was disappointed that a lot was left on the table. Fewer than 200 farmers opted for Track B, and even more disheartening was the fact that nearly 66,000 petitions were filed late and thus not heard.

There are myriad reasons why so many Black farmers did not step up to be heard or claim their due in the first Pigford case, many of which are discussed in greater and more nuanced detail in chapters fifteen and sixteen of this book. But the most straightforward one is that after so many years of broken promises, many Black farmers were simply too skeptical to believe their day had come. They could not believe the government really wanted to help them.

J.L. later said that if he had understood "the real magnitude of mistrust that hurting black farmers felt against their government I would have searched for some kind of formula specifically to address that problem."[37]

Hank was particularly frustrated that notices regarding the case didn't make it clear that descendants of farmers who had died were eligible in the settlement too. He was also concerned that the $50,000 amount per farmer wasn't adequate enough to qualify as justice. "When you take a farm away from people, you not only take away a way of earning a living, you also take away a lifestyle. Money can't replace that," he said in 2019.[38] The case was a beginning, though, and the settlement had confirmed that there was racism in the department and that Black farmers were harmed.

J. L. also blamed "people with secret motives and agendas" for the difficulties in deciding who was eligible, determining the settlement, and administering the payout. During the process, the court denied his request to name a Black lawyer as the monitor who kept track of all the claims. Furthermore, his objections to the government paying the salaries of those who were supposed to be independent and impartial—such as the mediator and the administrative judges, as well as the court-appointed monitor—were overruled.

When considering how to address the needs of the late claimants to the settlement, J. L. said he didn't think Pigford should be reopened. Because it was a court-approved binding contract between the Black farmer class and the government, he thought it would be simpler to file a new Pigford suit.

As J. L. would say about the first Pigford case while addressing a crowd of farmers in Albany, Georgia, in 2005, "Pigford was not perfect. No lawsuit or anything else crafted by the hand of man is perfect, because man is not perfect. But Pigford put more money in more Black hands in the shortest time than any lawsuit I've ever seen and I've been practicing law for 45 years. Pigford represents the only time in the history of the country that Congress passed a law (waiving the statute of limitations) to save a lawsuit filed by black folk or white folk for that matter—they haven't done that for white folk."[39]

J. L. urged the farmers to be proud. To be brave. To be determined. To be just like they were when they marched to the White House and the Capitol. Just like they were when they met with President Bill Clinton.

While appearing on MSNBC in 2013, Hank also reflected that Pigford was not just a Black farmer's case.[40] It was also a case about women, Hispanics, and Native Americans.[41]

Pigford II reopened the suit to the thousands of farmers who had filed late. Chestnut's firm had become Chestnut, Sanders, Sanders, Pettaway and Campbell, LLC by then.

J. L. Chestnut died in September 2008, just as Pigford II was underway. He was 77 years old. J. L. was brave and courageous, a warrior and a fighter, a groundbreaker and a smooth talker. In his obituary, *The New York Times* described him as an "underpublicized figure in the civil rights movement, a black man who began his career by taking on the ordinary legal briefs of ordinary black men and women, daring to work within the white establishment to achieve just ends."[42] He is a legendary figure in Alabama and should be a legendary figure in American history. Nearly a year later, in August 2009, a street in Selma named Jeff Davis Avenue—after the former president of the Confederate States of America during the Civil War—was renamed J. L. Chestnut Boulevard.

I remembered Rose, Hank's wife, suggesting that I petition to be lead counsel on the new Pigford case from my side. Chestnut and Sanders' firm would have to borrow about $2 million and narrow down to just three attorneys in order to keep the legal efforts going on their side. As Hank said years later, the case led to "financial disaster for the firm."[43] But it was never a project or a case. It was always a mission to take care of the farmers. Their firm petitioned to have Hank as lead counsel and my firm petitioned for me as suggested. Andy Marks of Coffey Burlington, who was in Washington, D.C., would become the liaison counsel. Hank and Andy had the Ivy League credentials. Hank went to Talladega and then Harvard. Andy went to Harvard for his undergraduate degree and then University of Michigan Law School. And then there was me, a guy who went to the University of Florida and was twenty-five years their junior. That's kind of a theme in my life. I just didn't realize then how stretching myself to fit the task was going to catapult my law practice and expand my life so fully.

PART TWO

———◦○◦○◦———

A SENSE OF HISTORY

CHAPTER FIVE

WHITE GOLD

INSOFAR AS THE LAND THAT MEN, WOMEN, AND CHILDREN TILLED over the centuries has fed and clothed the nation's populace—and at times, part of the world's populace—the history of Black farmers has bearing on the whole of the American identity, not just on Black identity. Of course, this history could fill a book, not just a few chapters in this one. But the stories that follow are the ones that even illiterate farmers knew to pass down to their children, grandchildren, and great-grandchildren in whatever ways they could. They're that important. Too important for you not to know as well.

About a dozen years after colonists first established Jamestown, the first permanent English settlement in the New World, a Portuguese slave ship, the *São João Bautista*, crossed the Atlantic Ocean with a hull full of kidnapped Africans, believed to be from Angola. According to historians, nearly half of them died at sea by the time two English pirate boats intercepted the death ship in 1619.

The English vessel *White Lion* took many of the remaining Africans to Point Comfort, a port on the James River in Virginia, where "20 and odd Negroes" or more were sold for food.[44] Some were taken to Jamestown, where they were sold once again. Three or four days later, the English ship *Treasurer* docked in Virginia, where its captain auctioned off another three or four more Africans.[45]

The first "muster," or census, of Virginia in March 1620 listed thirty-two Africans: seventeen women and fifteen men. Along with four Native Americans, they were described as "Others not Christians in the Service of the English."[46] They were the first African slaves to arrive in the American colonies, and, as we well know, millions more would follow them to the New World against their will.

For more than three centuries after the English colonists settled in Jamestown, farming was the backbone of America's economy. And for most of the first 250 years or so, slavery was the sinful mechanism that made it flourish. From cotton and tobacco plantations in the South to factories and banks in the North to textile mills in Great Britain, much of the world's economy was connected to the forced labor of enslaved African-Americans.

"Forced labor was not uncommon—Africans and Europeans had been trading goods and people across the Mediterranean for centuries—but enslavement had not been based on race," wrote Mary Elliott and Jazmine Hughes of *The New York Times Magazine*. "The trans-Atlantic slave trade, which began as early as the 15th century, introduced a system of slavery that was commercialized, racialized and inherited. Enslaved people were seen not as people at all but as commodities to be bought, sold and exploited. Though people of African descent—free and enslaved—were present in North America as early as the 1500s, the sale of the '20 and odd' African people set the course for what would become slavery in the United States."[47]

Even from the very first days at Plymouth Colony in Massachusetts in the early seventeenth century, farming was the means by which colonists grew food to eat, harvested fruits and vegetables to barter for meat, and how they traded with Native Americans for furs, which they sent back to Europe in exchange for tea, sugar, spices, oil, vinegar, shoes, clothes, gunpowder, and other staples.

The colonists at Plymouth called their settlement a "plantation," which came from the English word "plant." Since many of them traveled to the New World from large European cities, they had no experience in farming. If they were going to survive in the new land, however, they had to learn how to plant, cultivate, and harvest food in the shallow and sandy soil of coastal Massachusetts. The first Thanksgiving probably was not a bountiful feast as the tradition suggests. According to historians, their first crops were Indian corn, English barley, and a less-than-bumper crop of peas. Things got even leaner after that celebration, largely because of the colony's primitive tenant farming arrangement with the English merchants who had financed their transatlantic trips.

"For the next five years, the bread-and-butter problem was the all-absorbing problem at Plymouth. One reason was that when the Pilgrims had pledged themselves to work four days in the week for the merchants who financed their undertaking, it had been in the expectation that the latter would bear the real burden of supporting the Colony during its early years. But when they failed to receive adequate support from England, and ship after ship arrived bringing with it instead more mouths to feed, want, not to say starvation, soon stared them in the face."[48]

Fortunately for the Pilgrims, a formerly enslaved Native American named Squanto, who spoke English, brokered an alliance with a local tribe, the Wampanoag. Using herring and shad as fertilizer, the Native Americans taught the Pilgrims how to grow crops such as squash, corn, and beans in vast, open fields. In smaller gardens, women and children tended herbs and vegetables such as parsley, spinach, carrots, turnips, and lettuce. Eventually, the Pilgrims learned how to grow sweet potatoes, tomatoes, pumpkins, gourds, watermelon, berries, tobacco, and cotton.

After nearly starving to death, the Pilgrims also gave up their communist-style system of farming. "The big difficulty still remained: that of making profit for the Adventurers and at the same time earning enough to supply the colonists' own needs. So, since it was now clear that they could spend six days a week in the employ of the merchants only at the grave risk of starvation—inasmuch as no regular supplies of food were to be looked for from England—it was determined to abandon the work in common and to begin an entirely new system."[49]

Each man and family were allotted as much land as they could profitably use. Even in the early colonies, there was a distinct caste system: individual settlers received small land grants upon arriving. Larger and more fertile tracts of land were reserved for colonists who were politically connected. Beginning in the spring of 1623, there was a notable difference in work ethic and production for the farmers who were now working for themselves. "Everybody who had worked hard before worked harder now, and those who had not worked hard at all before began to do their share."[50]

Of course, indentured servants, who were at first poor Europeans, and then African slaves got nothing in return for their forced labor.

An early Virginia law affirmed the use of enslaved laborers; the 1662 law "decreed that the status of the child followed the status of the mother, which meant that enslaved women gave birth to generations of children of African descent who were now seen as commodities. This natural increase allowed the colonies—and then the United States—to become a slave nation. The law also secured wealth for European colonists and generations of their descendants, even as free black people could be legally prohibited from bequeathing their wealth to their children."[51] It is estimated that English importers alone enslaved more than three million Africans and brought them to the Americas. About 20 percent of the population of the thirteen colonies by the start of the American Revolutionary War in 1775 were enslaved Africans.[52]

Slave labor was used to plant, cultivate, and harvest tobacco and corn in Virginia; rice and indigo (an organic dye extracted from plant leaves) in Georgia and South Carolina; long-staple cotton in the Sea Islands of Georgia; short-staple cotton in multiple regions from South Carolina to Texas; and sugar in Florida, Georgia, and later in Louisiana and the lower parts of the Mississippi Valley.

No crop, however, had as much of an impact on the early American economy and its standing in the world as cotton. It made America a global economic and political power and sparked the nineteenth-century Industrial Revolution in the U.S. and Great Britain. While cotton had been used as a fiber in India and the Americas since at least 3000 B.C., and Christopher Columbus discovered it growing on the islands of the Bahamas before he landed in America, it is believed that cotton seeds were first planted in Florida by early settlers in the mid-sixteenth century. Colonists were growing white, fluffy bolls along the banks of the James River in Virginia by 1616.[53]

Sea Island cotton—a long-staple, black-seeded cotton that could be grown in warm climates and sandy soils near the coasts of the southern colonies—was superior to the types imported to Europe from the Middle East and India. Its long strands were good for spinning comfortable clothing and it was especially appealing because it didn't have to be combined with linen. In the early days, the cotton grown in America was mostly kept there for homespun clothing and other goods to meet everyday needs.

By the early eighteenth century, English factories began spinning cotton and a booming textile industry developed, supplying yarn, clothing, and other fabrics to the British Empire. Plantations across the Southern states in colonial America became the most important suppliers of cotton in the world. English inventions such as John Kay's flying shuttle in 1733 and James Hargreaves's spinning jenny in 1770 only increased the demand for "white gold."

Then in 1793, more than a decade after the thirteen colonies rebelled, won their independence from the British, and reopened their trade routes with the English, a young schoolteacher named Eli Whitney invented the automated cotton gin. The crude machine separated the seed from short-staple cotton nearly ten times faster than it could be done by hand.

The cotton gin increased output so dramatically in the U.S. that more land and additional labor was needed. In 1803, U.S. President Thomas Jefferson brokered the Louisiana Purchase with Napoleon Bonaparte and the French. For fifteen million dollars, the U.S. acquired nearly 830,000 square miles of land west of the Mississippi River, which nearly doubled the country's borders. The massive land acquisition also created a dearth of laborers.

Slavery had already become a moral issue in America, even though the founding fathers had largely ignored it while drafting the laws and papers that would shape the new democracy. Indeed, the promise written in the Declaration of Independence, "We hold these truths to be self-evident, that all men are created equal, that they are endowed by their Creator with certain unalienable Rights, that among these are Life, Liberty and the pursuit of Happiness," did not apply to the Black men, women, and children who had arrived in the United States as slaves, nor did it apply to their descendants.

Finally, in March 1807, Jefferson promoted a federal act to "prohibit the importation of slaves into any port or place within the jurisdiction of the United States ... from any foreign kingdom, place or country."[54] By the time the international slave trade ban took effect on January 1, 1808, every slave state besides South Carolina had abolished foreign slave trade.[55] Yet the act of owning slaves and domestic slave trading remained unimpeded. It is estimated that one million enslaved people were "sold down river" to Southern states to work on cotton, rice, and sugar fields after the Louisiana Purchase.[56]

By 1850, more than three million African-Americans were enslaved on Southern plantations, laboring in sunbaked fields for sixteen hours a day, six or seven days a week. It is estimated that 1.8 million of them worked in cotton fields.[57] "As demand for cotton grew and the nation expanded, slavery became more systemic, codified and regulated—as did the lives of all enslaved people," Elliott and Hughes wrote in *The New York Times Magazine*. "The sale of enslaved people and the products of their labor secured the nation's position as a global economic and political powerhouse, but they faced increasingly inhumane conditions. They were hired out to increase their worth, sold to pay off debts and bequeathed to the next generation. Slavery affected everyone, from textile workers, bankers and ship builders in the North; to the elite planter class, working-class slave catchers and slave dealers in the

South; to the yeoman farmers and poor white people who could not compete against free labor."[58]

Cotton planting typically occurred in the early spring, between March and April. During those months, slaves sowed seeds in straight rows, about three to five feet apart. From April until August, they weeded and tended plants. In early August, the entire plantation harvested the crop by hand. "Cotton picking occurred as many as seven times a season as the plant continued to flower and produce bolls through the fall and early winter. During the picking season, slaves worked from sunrise to sunset with a ten-minute break at lunch. Once they had brought the cotton to the gin house to be weighed, slaves then had to care for the animals and perform other chores."[59]

In the late 1850s, cotton from the U.S. accounted for "77 percent of the 800 million pounds of cotton consumed in Britain. It also accounted for 90 percent of the 192 million pounds used in France, 60 percent of the 115 million pounds spun in the Zollverein, and 92 percent of the 102 million pounds manufactured in Russia."[60] Raw cotton was responsible for 61 percent of the value of all U.S. products shipped abroad, and by 1860 the antebellum South produced two-thirds of the world's cotton.[61]

It is estimated that "in 1862, fully 20 million people worldwide—one out of every 65 people alive—were involved in the cultivation of cotton or the production of cotton cloth. In England alone, which still counted two-thirds of the world's mechanical spindles in its factories, the livelihood of between one-fifth and one-fourth of the population was based on the industry, one-tenth of all British capital was invested in it, and close to one-half of all exports consisted of cotton yarn and cloth."[62]

———— • ————

While Southerners defended slavery and their "way of life," abolitionists in the North worked tirelessly to end it. On November 6, 1860, Kentucky-born lawyer Abraham Lincoln, a member of the anti-slavery Republican party, was elected the sixteenth president of the United

States. He had been defeated in a Senate race two years earlier after arguing against the spread of slavery.

A month after Lincoln was elected president, South Carolina seceded from the Union, citing "an increasing hostility on the part of the nonslaveholding states to the institution of slavery" as a cause.[63] By the time Lincoln was inaugurated on March 4, 1861, a total of seven states had seceded, formed the Confederate States of America, and elected Jefferson Davis as president. A month later, General P. G. T. Beauregard and his Confederate troops fired on Union-held Fort Sumter in South Carolina, starting the American Civil War.

There were several events that ultimately contributed to the emancipation of millions of Black slaves in the Confederate states. The Fugitive Slave Law of 1850 required that escaped slaves had to be returned to their owners. The law made Union generals unsure of what to do with African-Americans who had escaped slavery by crossing into Union lines during the war.

In May 1861, Union major general Benjamin Butler, an abolitionist and lawyer from Massachusetts, provided shelter and safety to three fugitive slaves at Fort Monroe, near what is now Hampton, on the southern tip of the Virginia peninsula. When a Confederate colonel arrived at the fort and demanded his slaves be returned, Butler refused to do so. He argued that because Virginia had seceded from the Union, the Fugitive Slave Law of 1850 no longer protected citizens' property there. Butler took it a step further and declared that the escaped slaves should be considered "contraband of war" because they were being used in helping the Confederate war effort. Soon, hundreds of slaves fled to Fort Monroe for Butler's protection. Many of them became spies and laborers for the Union army.

That August, the Senate passed the Confiscation Act, which was designed to allow the federal government to seize property, including slaves who were being used to support the Confederate war effort.[64] Lincoln signed the bill into law, but it proved to be nothing more than symbolic. In fact, Lincoln continued to push back on Union efforts to emancipate slaves.

On August 30, 1861, John C. Frémont, the Union commander of the Department of the West, issued a proclamation that emancipated all slaves being held by rebels or Southern sympathizers in the border state of Missouri. "The property, real and personal, of all persons in the State of Missouri, who shall take up arms against the United States, or who shall be directly proven to have taken an active part with their enemies in the field, is declared to be confiscated to their public use, and their slaves, if any they have, are hereby declared freemen."[65]

Frémont also declared martial law and warned that every captured and armed Rebel would be court-martialed and shot if guilty. Lincoln believed the act was too radical and might turn Missouri to the Confederacy, so he ordered Frémont to rescind his order. When Frémont refused, Lincoln removed him from his command. "Though the president would ultimately force him to rescind the order, Frémont, in declaring that the war for the Union was by necessity a war against slavery, amplified abolitionism as war policy, opening a road that would never be closed."[66]

When it became clear that most Northerners supported confiscating Confederate property, Senator Lyman Trumbull of Illinois introduced a second Confiscation Act, in December 1861, to allow the seizure of all Confederate property, whether it had been used in the war or not. Radical Republicans wanted to pass the bill to free all slaves, while moderates worried that the federal government would be overreaching and denying property owners their constitutional rights. A compromised bill permitted the federal government to free slaves in conquered Rebel territory, prohibited the return of fugitive slaves, and allowed the Union Army to recruit newly freed African-Americans. While even that bill wasn't fully enforced, it opened the door for Lincoln's Emancipation Proclamation.

The following March, Union major general David Hunter took control of the Department of the South and promptly captured Fort Pulaski near Hilton Head, South Carolina. On April 25, 1862, Hunter, a longtime abolitionist, issued General Order No. 11, in which he proclaimed that slaves in Georgia, South Carolina, and Florida were free: "The three States of Georgia, Florida and South Carolina, comprising the military department of the south, having deliberately declared themselves no longer under the protection of the United States of America, and having taken up arms against the said United States, it becomes a military necessity to declare them under martial law. This was accordingly done on the 25th day of April, 1862. Slavery and martial law in a free country are altogether incompatible; the persons in these three States—Georgia, Florida, and South Carolina—heretofore held as slaves, are therefore declared forever free."[67]

Shortly thereafter, Hunter formed the 1st South Carolina Voluntary Infantry Regiment (African Descent), which was among the first officially recognized Black units of the Union Army. Once again, concerned about disenfranchising slaveholding residents in the border states, Lincoln soon ordered the regiment be disbanded and Hunter's emancipation be rescinded.

As the U.S. prepared for its third year of war, Lincoln delivered the preliminary Emancipation Proclamation on September 22, 1862. In it, he vowed that if the Confederate states did not end their uprising by the New Year, "all persons held as slaves" within the rebellious states "are, and henceforward shall be free."[68] It didn't free all slaves, however, as it applied only to states that had seceded and did not impact loyal slaveholding states such as Delaware, Kentucky, Maryland, and Missouri. It also did not apply to slaves being held in Confederate states that were already under Union control.[69]

The bloody war, which killed an estimated 360,222 men from the North and 258,000 from the South, finally ended on April 9, 1865, when Confederate General Robert E. Lee surrendered at Appomattox.[70] On December 6, 1865, nearly 250 years after the "20 and odd Negroes" were sold in Virginia, the 13th Amendment was ratified, abolishing slavery in the U.S. It states: "Neither slavery nor involuntary servitude, except as a punishment for crime whereof the party shall have been duly convicted, shall exist within the United States, or any place subject to their jurisdiction."[71] The freedom that Lincoln promised finally came for enslaved Blacks.

With the war and slavery in America finally over, freed Blacks began their fight to own land and gain the same civil rights and economic rewards as Whites who once "owned" them. It was a biblical battle that would last for more than a century—and, in so many ways, is still being fought today.

CHAPTER SIX

———◆———

FORTY ACRES AND A MULE

ON JANUARY 12, 1865—ELEVEN MONTHS BEFORE THE 13ᵗʰ AMENDMENT was ratified—Union General William T. Sherman, who had just completed his destructive March to the Sea through Georgia, and Secretary of War Edwin Stanton met with local Black leaders in the coastal city of Savannah.

The Black group's leader was Reverend Garrison Frazier, a Baptist minister, who had been a slave only eight years earlier. He paid one thousand dollars in gold and silver to buy freedom for his wife and himself. He explained slavery like this: "Slavery is, receiving by *irresistible power* the work of another man, and not by his *consent*. The freedom, as I understand it ...is taking us from under the yoke of bondage, and placing us where we could reap the fruit of our own labor ....The way we can best take care of ourselves is to have land, and turn it and till it by our own labor ...and we can soon maintain ourselves and have something to spare."[72]

During that meeting in Savannah, Sherman and Stanton asked Frazier whether the newly freed men, and their families, would prefer to live scattered among the Whites or in colonies among themselves. According to Sherman's notes from the meeting, Frazier responded: "I would prefer to live by ourselves, for there is a prejudice against us in the South that will take years to get over."[73]

Four days later, Sherman issued Special Field Order No. 15, in which he commanded that 400,000 acres of coastal property the Union had confiscated from Confederate landowners be redistributed to Black families in forty-acre plots. In the order, among other things, Sherman promised:

"The islands from Charleston, south, the abandoned rice fields along the rivers for thirty miles back from the sea, and the country bordering the St. Johns river, Florida, are reserved and set apart for the settlement of the Negroes now made free by the acts of war and the proclamation of the President of the United States.

II. At Beaufort, Hilton Head, Savannah, Fernandina, St. Augustine and Jacksonville, the Blacks may remain in their chosen or accustomed vocations—but on the islands, and in the settlements hereafter to be established, no white person whatever, unless military officers and soldiers detailed for duty, will be permitted to reside; and the sole and exclusive management of affairs will be left to the freed people themselves, subject only to the United States military authority and the acts of Congress."[74]

Sherman's plan addressed two big problems America would face during Reconstruction: what to do with the newly freed slaves and how to punish the Confederate landowners for their roles in the rebellion. The U.S. government had considered drastic action to resettle the newly freed slaves. President Abraham Lincoln proposed colonizing the former slaves in Panama as coal mine laborers for the Chiriqui Improvement Company.[75] Another plan involved colonizing the freedmen on an island off the coast of Haiti, and yet another settled more than 2,500 former slaves in Liberia.[76]

Remarkably, many freedmen didn't want to leave the country that had enslaved them for so many years. In August 1865, a convention of freemen in Virginia declared: "That as natives of American soil we claim the right to remain upon it, and that any attempt to remove, expatriate, or colonize us in any other land against our will is unjust, for here we were born, and for this country our fathers and brothers have fought, and we hope to remain here in the full enjoyment of enfranchised manhood and its dignities."[77]

Reconstruction was an anguished time for the four million former slaves, who had no homes or jobs and little to no education. What exactly was freedom for them? What did it mean going forward? Was it simply not being a slave or was it more?

While Northern abolitionists had worked tirelessly to help free the slaves, not enough effort went into planning how to help them transition to freedom and independence. Many of the freedmen wanted to become farmers, because it was the only occupation they had known, but the government had not established a method for them to acquire land and buy the animals, tools, and seed needed to become self-sufficient.

"At that time, life for most of the four million freed black people was desperate as they pushed away from the South and slave plantations with no clear idea of where to go and often with no food. In the words of abolitionist Harriet Tubman, 'I was free, but there was no one to welcome me to the land of freedom—I was a stranger in a strange land.' Many of the former slaves eventually returned to their old plantations, their spirits broken. They resumed working as field hands on farms, laboring under the same conditions as they had when they were slaves."[78]

Yet others took advantage of Sherman's promise. He appointed Brigadier General Rufus Saxton to divvy up the land. While it wasn't part of Sherman's order, some Black landowners also received retired Army mules to help them plow. In the first six months after Sherman issued his special order, forty thousand Black people had relocated to more than 400,000 acres of farmland on the coasts of Florida, Georgia, and the Sea Islands of South Carolina.[79]

In March 1865, Congress authorized Sherman to lease the land and supply plow mules to the new farmers. The rent the Black farmers paid helped establish the Bureau of Refugees, Freedmen, and Abandoned Lands (the Freedmen's Bureau) in the U.S. War Department. The Freedmen's Bureau provided assistance to former slaves and poor Whites in the Southern states, where Union armies had destroyed cities, towns, and plantations during the Civil War.

Under the guidance of Major General Oliver O. Howard, the Freedmen's Bureau distributed food and clothing, operated hospitals and temporary camps, and opened more than four thousand Black schools, including Atlanta University (now Clark Atlanta), Fisk University, and Howard University. The Bureau helped Blacks find employment, locate family members, legalize marriages, and assisted veterans of color. It is estimated that the Freedmen's Bureau provided medical assistance to more than one million people and distributed more than twenty-one million rations to poor Blacks and Whites displaced by the war and emancipation.[80]

The Freedmen's Bureau also assumed the responsibility of establishing legal courts that would adjudicate criminal and civil cases involving Blacks, as well as oversee their treatment in state and local courts. The Bureau mediated contract negotiations between former slaves and landowners, ensured planters paid them fairly and on time, and arbitrated disputes whenever they arose.

"In this atmosphere of fear, poverty, and confusion, the promise of 'Forty Acres and a Mule' was seen as a sign of God's own deliverance," the political commentator Juan Williams wrote in an essay in the book *Black Farmers in America*. "The offer created a sensation among the nation's black population, which reacted as if Moses had parted the waters to the Promised Land. They could finally see a place in America where they could be self-sufficient and determine their own future."[81]

For freed Blacks, this meant breaking the chains of White control. It meant having the freedom to own land, legalize marriages, reunite with parents, spouses, and children who might have been "sold down the river," and to make other important decisions on their own. It meant being able to learn to read and write, to attend school, and establish colleges and universities for African-Americans.

For White Southerners, whose families had relied on free labor for more than a century, the development was troublesome. They viewed the former enslaved Blacks as unprepared and incapable of handling the new freedoms the government was affording them. The former Confederate states resented the Union and the Freedmen's Bureau ruling their land. Southerners also feared their agricultural economy would collapse without the labor of the millions of newly freed men and women.

"Why was it that the vast majority of former slaves never got the chance to own land in the period after the Civil War?" asked Katherine C. Mooney, in the foreword of the 2011 edition of Louisiana State University professor Claude F. Oubre's book *Forty Acres and A Mule*. "Despite some attempts by both military and civilian authorities to settle black families on their own land, most of them, at the end of Reconstruction, remained landless. Without land, Oubre argued, they were more vulnerable to the threats of white men intent on returning them to a subordination as close as possible to the slavery now rendered unconstitutional. In slavery, their labor had made the land of the South one of the most prosperous agricultural empires of all time, but they were denied any right to the ground their labor had made bountiful."[82]

Then, on April 14, 1865, five days after the Civil War ended, Southern sympathizer John Wilkes Booth shot President Lincoln in the back of the head at Ford's Theatre in Washington, D.C. Lincoln died the next morning. Vice President Andrew Johnson, a former governor and senator from Tennessee, assumed the presidency. Johnson sought to restore the seceded states to the Union as quickly as possible, regardless of what happened to the former slaves. Johnson lobbied for amnesty for former Confederate soldiers and officials, many of whom had returned home and demanded the government give back their land.

During the following year, Southern states held constitutional conventions and elections in which many Confederate leaders and former slave owners won positions in state governments and the U.S. Congress. Although they had to pledge loyalty to the Union and repay war debts, Southerners were given near autonomy by the federal government while rebuilding their states during Reconstruction.

Soon, Southern states began passing discriminatory laws, known as Black Codes, which applied only to Black people and limited the former slaves' civil rights. For the first time, taxpayers in the South funded public education, but laws prohibited Black children from attending the schools. Blacks were not allowed to vote, serve as jurors, nor carry firearms and other weapons. Mississippi was the first state to propose such codes in late 1865, including a Vagrancy Law, which stated:

> "*Be it further enacted,* that all freedmen, free Negroes, and mulattoes in this state over the age of eighteen years found on the second Monday in January 1866, or thereafter, with no lawful employment or business, or found unlawfully assembling themselves together either in the day or nighttime, and all white persons so assembling with freedmen, free Negroes, or mulattoes, or usually associating with freedmen, free Negroes, or mulattoes on terms of equality, or living in adultery or fornication with a freedwoman, free Negro, or mulatto, shall be deemed vagrants; and, on conviction thereof, shall be fined in the sum of not exceeding, in the case of a freedman, free Negro, or mulatto, $150, and a white man, $200, and imprisoned at the discretion of the court, the free Negro not exceeding ten days, and the white man not exceeding six months ...."[83]

In Mississippi, a Black person was guilty of a felony and faced life in prison if they married a White. Each January, the law required Blacks to have written evidence of employment for the coming year. If they quit before the end of the term of employment, they could be jailed and would have to forfeit wages they had already earned. If they couldn't prove employment, they could be fined, arrested, or even leased back to their former slave owners.

The South Carolina "Black Code" law that was passed in December 1865 was even more restrictive and offensive. The law stated that all persons of color who had labor contracts would be known as "servants" and their employers would be known as "masters."

"On farms or in out-door service, the hours of labor, except on Sunday, shall be from sun-rise to sun-set, with a reasonable interval for breakfast and dinner," the South Carolina law stated. "Servants shall rise at the dawn in the morning, feed, water and care for the animals on the farm, do the usual and needful work about the premises, prepare their meals for the day, if required by the master, and begin the farm work or other work by sun-rise. The servant shall be careful of all the animals and property of his master, and especially of the animals and implements used by him, shall protect the same from injury by other persons, and shall be answerable for all property lost, destroyed or injured by his negligence, dishonesty or bad faith."[84]

South Carolina also proposed a law that prohibited Blacks from working any job other than as a farmer or a servant, unless they paid an annual tax ranging from ten dollars to one hundred dollars. "No person of color shall pursue or practice the art, trade or business of an artisan, mechanic or shop-keeper, or any other trade, employment or business (besides that of husbandry, or that of a servant under a contract for service or labor), on his own account and for his own benefit, or in partnership with a white person, or as agent or servant of any persons, until he shall have obtained a license therefore from the Judge of the District Court; which license shall be good for one year only."[85]

In South Carolina and other Southern states, apprenticeship laws authorized courts to "apprentice" Black orphans and children of "vagrants or destitute parents" to employers until females turned 18 and males turned 21. While some codes required the employers to teach the children a trade, feed and clothe them, and send them to school, it also provided the White farmers free labor. The South Carolina law permitted employers to "moderately" whip servants under 18; a judge's order was required to whip adult servants.[86]

Black Code laws in Mississippi, South Carolina, and other Southern states enraged Northern abolitionists, who accused White Southerners of attempting to restore slavery. Union military governors and the Freedmen's Bureau rescinded the Black Code laws in Mississippi and

South Carolina. Fearing that the North would assume control of the states, the elected officials revised and softened their codes.[87]

————•————

President Johnson's desire for amnesty for former Confederate soldiers and officials hampered the Freedmen's Bureau's efforts to settle former slaves and their families on confiscated land. "Senator Lyman Trumbull of Illinois, one of the architects of the Fourteenth Amendment, urged his colleagues to extend the life of the Bureau and its power to grant land and startup supplies to free men and their families. Bureau agents on the ground sometimes worked feverishly to circumvent amnesty proclamations, getting irreversible title to the land into black hands before the government could be forced to turn it back over to white planters."[88]

Saxton, Howard, and others also tried to secure land ownership for Black farmers despite Johnson's amnesty plans. If their efforts had worked, according to one historian, ". . . as many as 900,000 acres of plantation lands previously belonging to slave owners might have been redistributed."[89] When Johnson ordered Howard to return plantation owners much of the land that Sherman had promised to the freedmen, Howard tried to reach a compromise with the former slaves who believed they were entitled to the land their families had worked for generations. Their response to Howard, who had lost his arm in the Battle of Fair Oaks in Virginia:

"You ask us to forgive the landowners of our island. You only lost your right arm in the war and might forgive them. The man who tied me to a tree and gave me 39 lashes; who stripped and flogged my mother & sister & . . . who combines with others to keep away land from me . . . that man, I cannot well forgive. Does it look as if he has forgiven me, since he tries to keep me in a condition of helplessness?"[90]

According to author and historian Rick Beard, the Freedmen's Bureau controlled 223,600 acres on January 31, 1866. Within eighteen months, that total had decreased to just 75,329 acres. Within a year of the Civil War ending, the Freedmen's Bureau had turned over 400,000 acres to the plantation owners.[91]

In the summer of 1866, Congress passed the Southern Homestead Act, which reserved more than forty-six million acres of unsettled public land in Alabama, Arkansas, Florida, Louisiana, and Mississippi for freedmen and their families. It was an extension of Lincoln's 1862 Homestead Act, which opened up the American West to settlers and forced Native Americans off their ancestral land and into reservations. The 1862 Homestead Act resulted in 1.6 million deeds in thirty states, including Colorado, Montana, Nebraska, and North Dakota.[92]

However, there was one caveat with the Southern Homestead Act: former slaves had until January 1, 1867 to settle an eighty-acre tract. After farming the land for five years, the government would allow the African-Americans to buy the farms for a small fee. But since many Southern states required freedmen to sign one-year contracts with planters, they were unable to quit their jobs and move to another area without the risk of losing their earnings and potentially being arrested and jailed for breaking their contracts. What's more, many White planters feared that they would lose their laborers and tenant farmers, so they failed to inform their workers about the new Homestead Act. Even former slaves who did know about it, simply could not afford the nominal sum needed to acquire the land, much of which was swamp and forest that wasn't suitable for farming anyway.

The Southern Homestead Act ended up being a complete failure. The bureaucracy and tangle of administrative paperwork posed too many obstacles. "They were particularly difficult for people usually without cash resources or experience in dealing with men behind desks who were disinclined to be helpful. The land offices to which blacks had to travel to get their paperwork settled were simply not open for months at a time. Sometimes, a state had only one land office, and it cost more for a prospective farmer to travel there than the cost of his entire acreage under the Act."[93]

In 1867, the government started to allow Southern Whites to obtain the land. It wasn't the last time the federal government would utilize artificial barriers and administrative obstacles to prevent Blacks from acquiring land and services needed for financial security. Nor was it the last time that the spoils would go to Whites.

Seeing that the Freedmen's Bureau and U.S. Treasury Department had limited success assisting even those African-Americans who did have cash savings to purchase or lease land, a group of 130 former slaves pooled their resources and leased Confederate General Richard Taylor's plantation, known as Fashion, which Union forces had plundered and burned to the ground.[94] General Taylor, the son of President Zachary Taylor, never attempted to regain control of his 1,200-acre sugarcane plantation, which was located about thirty miles upriver from New Orleans.

Another successful colonization of former slaves occurred in Warren County, Mississippi. In 1818, lawyer Joseph Emory Davis established Davis Bend when he purchased about 11,000 acres of swampland along the Mississippi River twenty miles south of Vicksburg. In 1835, Davis sold a portion of this land to his youngest brother, Jefferson, who Southerners elected as the first president of the Confederacy. Fearing the plantation would be confiscated by the Union, and with his brother imprisoned at the time, Joseph Davis sold the land to Benjamin Montgomery, an African-American he had enslaved for twenty-nine years. Montgomery, an overseer and owner of the plantation store, paid $300,000 in gold at 6 percent interest.[95]

Davis Bend thereby became one of the first all-Black communities following the war, and with the help of many of Davis's former slaves, Montgomery and his sons built a highly successful cotton operation. Davis Bend produced award-winning long-staple cotton, which took first place at the St. Louis Fair in 1870 and later at expositions in Cincinnati and Philadelphia. At one point, the Montgomery family employed one thousand field hands.[96]

But this hint of prosperity was halted before its seeds could even spread. On Christmas Day 1868, President Johnson issued pardons to all Confederate soldiers who fought in the Civil War. After extending "unconditionally, and without reservation ... a full pardon and amnesty for the offence [sic] of treason against the United States, or of adhering to their enemies during the late Civil War, with restoration of all rights, privileges, and immunities under the Constitution and the laws." He explained that his action was intended to "renew and fully restore confidence and fraternal feeling among the whole, and their respect for and attachment to the National Government, designed by its patriotic founders for the general good."[97]

With those pardons, Johnson returned much of the confiscated land that the government was supposed to redistribute to African-Americans to help them establish self-sufficiency. Two years earlier, Johnson had vetoed a bill that would have extended the life of the Freedmen's Bureau and given it greater legal powers. He argued then that it interfered with states' rights and gave preference to one group of citizens over another. He also cut funding to the Bureau and removed employees he considered to be too sympathetic to Blacks. Finally, under pressure from White Southerners, the federal government shuttered the Freedmen's Bureau in the summer of 1872.

And with that, the promise of "Forty Acres and a Mule" as reparations evaporated into thin air. As Juan Williams has so eloquently written, "The offer of 'Forty Acres and a Mule' vanished into the status of legend, becoming a catch-phrase for all the broken promises the government has ever made to black people."[98]

The abolitionist Frederick Douglass wondered what might have happened to Blacks if Johnson hadn't forced the freedmen off their land.

"Could the nation have been induced to listen to those stalwart Republicans, Thaddeus Stevens and Charles Sumner," Douglass wrote in 1880, "some of the evils which we now suffer would have been averted. The negro would not today be on his knees ... supplicating the old master class to give him leave to toil ... [And] he would not now be swindled out of his hard earnings."[99]

CHAPTER SEVEN

———◆———

A NEW KIND OF SLAVERY

URING THE SUMMER OF 1903, A LETTER ARRIVED AT THE WHITE House for U.S. President Theodore Roosevelt. The handwritten correspondence was authored by a Black woman named Carrie Kinsey, who pleaded for Roosevelt's help in freeing her 14-year-old brother, James Robinson. She claimed he had been sold to a plantation owner in Georgia. She made her desperate appeal more than four decades after President Abraham Lincoln delivered the Emancipation Proclamation, in which he declared "that all persons held as slaves" within the Confederate states "are, and henceforward shall be free."

In the letter, which has been slightly altered to correct spelling and include punctuation, Kinsey wrote:

> "Mr. President I have a brother about 14 years old. A colored man came here and hired him from me, and said that he would take good care of him, and pay me five dollars a month for him—and I

heard of him no more. He went and sold him to McRee, and they has been working him in prison for 12 months and I has tried to get them to send him to me and they won't let him go. He has no mother and no father. They are both dead, and I am his only friend and they won't let me have him. He has not done nothing for them to have him in chains, so I write to you for you to help me get my poor brother. His name is James Robinson. And the man that carried him off, his name is Dan Cal. He sold him to McCree at Valdosta, Georgia. Please let me hear from you at once."[100]

According to records at the National Archives, President Roosevelt probably never read Kinsey's letter. It was forwarded to the U.S. Justice Department, which filed it away with thousands of more like it. Douglas A. Blackmon, the author of the Pulitzer Prize-winning book *Slavery by Another Name: The Re-Enslavement of Black Americans from the Civil War to World War II*, discovered that Robinson had probably been sold into involuntary servitude with hundreds of other Black men and boys at a plantation called Kinderlou in Valdosta.[101]

Kinderlou, which covered about 22,000 acres, produced cotton, tobacco, sugarcane, tomatoes, watermelons, cantaloupes, and corn. Edward McRee, a member of the Georgia legislature, and his brothers, William and Frank, owned the plantation. Their father, George McRee, had been a Confederate officer. Kinderlou had its own railroad stop, where laborers loaded crates of produce onto boxcars, and where cotton gins and steam engines necessary to ground sugarcane into syrup were delivered. The McRees also produced thousands of wood pallets and crates to ship their produce across the South.[102]

"Initially, the McRees hired only free black labor, but beginning in the 1890s they routinely leased a hundred or more convicts from the state of Georgia to perform the grueling work of clearing land, removing stumps, ditching fields, and constructing roads," Blackmon wrote. "Other prisoners hoed, plowed, and weeded the crops. Over the course of fifteen years, thousands of men and women were forced to Kinderlou and held in stockades under the watch of armed guards. After the turn of the century, the brothers began to arrange for even more forced laborers through the sheriffs of nearby counties in Georgia and Florida—fueling what eventually grew into a sprawling traffic in humans."[103]

Remarkably, Blackmon uncovered tens of thousands of pages of documents at the National Archives that detailed largely unanswered complaints to the federal government of involuntary servitude and forced labor in the Deep South following the Civil War.

"As dumbfounding as the story told by the Carrie Kinsey letter is, far more remarkable is what surrounds that letter at the National Archives," Blackmon wrote in *Washington Monthly* magazine. "In the same box that holds her grief-stricken missive are at least half a dozen other pieces of correspondence recounting other stories of kidnapping, perversion of the courts, or human trafficking—as horrifying as, or worse than, Carrie Kinsey's tale. It is the same in the next box on the shelf. And the one before. And the ones on either side of those. And the next and the next. And on and on. Thousands and thousands of plaintive letters and grimly bureaucratic responses—altogether at least 30,000 pages of original material—chronicle cases of forced labor and involuntary servitude in the South decades after the end of the Civil War."[104]

Among the other notes Blackmon found was a letter Reverend L.R. Farmer of Morganton, North Carolina, penned after his daughter had been kidnapped.

"Dear Sir, i write you for information i have a little girl that has been kidnapped from me and is now under bondage in Ga and I cant get her out only her but no of others i want ask you is it law for people to whip (col) people and keep them and not allow them to leave without a pass ...."[105]

For more than seventy-five years after the Civil War, hundreds of thousands of Black people were systematically forced to work in the former Confederate states, whether it was through peonage, sharecropping, convict leasing, or chain gangs.

The Deep South's economy was in ruins following the war. White planters were confronted with two primary challenges. They had lost their wealth and their labor force when four million African-American slaves were freed. So they had to rebuild and now they had to pay their laborers to keep their plantations operating. Once the federal government withdrew from the South following Reconstruction in 1877, corruption and Black oppression flourished as White Southerners attempted to keep their economy and society intact.

Blackmon and other historians have meticulously documented how corrupt plantation owners, sheriffs, lawyers, and even judges conspired to charge Blacks with petty crimes they didn't commit, convict them without trials, and then enslave them to planters, lumber companies, and other industrialists who paid their bail or fines. Cities, counties, and states were willing parties to this fraud because the fees they were paid for convict leases saved them money on clothing, feeding, and housing the "prisoners." The Black laborers were forced to work for months or years to settle their debts, which were oftentimes compounded by charges for being housed, clothed, and fed while enslaved. Some laborers spent the rest of their lives working off their debt.

Georgia, for example, approved the leasing of prisoners—nearly all of them African-Americans—within three years of the Civil War ending. Thomas Ruger, the provisional governor, approved the first convict lease of one hundred Black prisoners to William A. Fort of the Georgia and the Alabama Railroad on May 11, 1868. The company was charged $2,500 for one year. Sixteen of the prisoners died during that time.[106] By 1869, the state had leased out each of the 393 prisoners from the state prison in Milledgeville. During an eighteen-month period in 1872 and 1873, the state generated more than $35,000 from prison labor.[107] When increased media attention exposed the harsh treatment of prisoners, the state legislature abolished convict leasing in 1908. Chain gangs persisted in the state until the mid-1940s.

In Alabama, convict leasing started in 1875 following a statewide financial crisis. As the state looked for more revenue streams, warden John G. Bass launched a program that leased state prisoners to coal mines, farms, and lumber companies. The state made between $11,000 to $12,000 in the first year.[108] Eight years later, nearly all state or county prisoners were working under convict-leasing arrangements in coal mines around Birmingham. Many of them were transported directly to worksites following their convictions. In 1928, Alabama became the last state in the country to abolish convict leasing; Florida had halted the controversial practice about five years earlier.[109]

Peonage, which is defined as debt slavery or debt servitude, was outlawed by Congress in 1867 and upheld by the U.S. Supreme Court in 1905. Yet the system of compelling laborers to work with minimal or no pay wasn't completely eradicated in the South until the 1940s. Planters and other employers deceived Blacks into signing labor contracts—sometimes for ten years or longer—to pay their debts and avoid fines that courts might have imposed. Cartels conspired to keep wages low and ensure that planters refrained from hiring others' workers for higher pay.

Kinderlou is the perfect example of how the corruption worked. In his 1977 book *Black Georgia in the Progressive Era, 1900-1920*, historian John Dittmer noted that Sheriff Thomas J. McClellan of Waycross, Georgia, arrested and charged a Black woman named Lula Frazier on an adultery charge in the summer of 1902.[110] McClellan suggested that Frazier hire attorney William F. Crawley to defend her. Even after the city attorney refused to prosecute Frazier because she was legally married to Nathan Frazier, the man named on her adultery complaint, McClellan refused to release her. Around that time, Crawley wired Edward McRee a brief message: "Come to Waycross for woman."[111]

As one of McRee's brothers boarded a train for Waycross, Crawley and McClellan lied to Frazier and told her that she had been convicted. They informed her that she could pay a fifty-dollar fine or spend a year working on the county chain gang. There was one more option they offered to her: Edward McRee would pay her fine in exchange for her working eighteen months for him. At Kinderlou, according to Dittmer, Frazier was "beaten, locked up at night, and sexually assaulted. After she had worked there nine months her husband and a new sheriff obtained her release."[112]

Dittmer also documented how Crawley arranged for two Black boys, Henry Brimmage and David Smith of Ware County, Georgia, to work seven months at Kinderlou after they were convicted of stealing a watermelon in August 1903. In that case, Edward McRee agreed to pay sixty-five dollars for Crawley's attorney fees and McClellan's jail expenses in exchange for the boys' labor.[113] A 15-year-old Black woman, Lula Durham, spent three months at Kinderlou after a Black doctor accused her of having "immoral conduct with a young man and threatened to prosecute unless she paid him twenty-five dollars."[114]

In the summer of 1903, an assistant U.S. attorney in Macon, Georgia, opened an investigation into McRee's sprawling operation. That November, the federal government indicted McRee and his brothers, as well as Crawley, McClellan, and other plantation owners, on charges of peonage and "holding certain men, women and children of the colored race in involuntary servitude." The McRees were charged with thirteen counts of enslaving African-American men and women.

Three plantation owners near Zaidee, Georgia, were charged with violating the Thirteenth Amendment, which outlawed slavery and involuntary servitude, stating "they put the negroes under the lash, maltreated them, and inflicted bodily injury, at the same time forcibly and by confinement keeping them in slavery."[115]

At the federal courthouse in Savannah, Georgia, Edward McRee assured a judge that he and his brothers never intended to enslave anyone. "Though we are probably technically guilty we did not know it," he told the court. "This custom has been [in] existence ever since the war .... We never knew that we were doing anything wrong."[116]

Federal Judge Emory Speer allowed McRee and his brothers to plead guilty to two of the thirteen charges and pay fines of only $1,000. The judge dismissed the charges in the other cases. Speer later told the McRees that he could have fined them $260,000 and sentenced them to sixty-five years in prison.[117] Crawley and McClellan pleaded guilty to four counts, and Speer sentenced them to $1,000 fines but no jail time. He reduced their fines to five hundred dollars the same day, according to Dittmer.[118]

The McRee trial was typical of many peonage cases in the South, so much so that federal prosecutors and judges largely ignored the issue in the early part of the twentieth century. But a 1911 ruling by the U.S. Supreme Court invalidated an Alabama peonage law, which criminalized a worker breaking his labor contract after receiving an advance payment from his employer. That widespread practice made it more difficult for Black laborers to find better opportunities. Another Supreme Court ruling three years later struck down Southern states' criminal surety laws, which allowed planters and other employers to pay bail and court-imposed fines and then have workers pay off the debt through labor. The high court ruled that "convicts held under 'criminal contracts' to work out their fines and costs with persons who appear in court as their financial sponsors were held in peonage."[119]

Yet the Supreme Court rulings did little to change the peonage system in the South. As a result, laborers who escaped were chased down by bloodhounds, arrested again, fined even more money, and then sent back to the same plantations. Others who objected to their paltry pay, minimal food, and cramped living conditions were severely beaten. Men and women who fought back were sent to work on the chain gang or murdered.

In May 1918, not far from Kinderlou in Brooks County, Georgia, a White plantation owner named Hampton Smith was shot and killed. A White mob suspected the assailant was Sidney Johnson, a 19-year-old worker who was paying off a thirty-dollar debt after he was arrested for rolling dice. Johnson ran from the plantation. Over the course of next two weeks the mob killed thirteen other Black people they also suspected of playing a role in Smith's murder.

Among the victims was Hazel "Hayes" Turner. When Turner's wife, Mary, a 19-year-old Black woman who was eight months pregnant, threatened to swear out a warrant against her husband's murderers, the mob went after her. When she was found at Folsom Bridge, over the Little River, which separated Brooks County from Lowndes County, the mob tied her ankles, strung her upside down in a tree, doused her with gasoline and motor oil, and set her afire. What happened next was even more horrific.

Walter White, an official with the National Association for the Advancement of Colored People, went to Brooks County to investigate the killings. He wrote about Mary Turner's brutal murder in a 1929 book: "Mocking, ribald laughter from her tormenters answered the helpless woman's screams of pain and terror. 'Mister, you ought to've heard the nigger wench howl!' a member of the mob boasted to me a few days later .... The clothes [having] burned from her crisply toasted body in which, unfortunately, life still lingered, a man stepped towards the woman and, with his knife, ripped open the abdomen in a crude Caesarean operation. Out tumbled the prematurely born child. Two feeble cries it gave—and received for answer the heel of a stalwart man, as life was ground out of the tiny form."[120]

Turner and her baby were buried nearby in a shallow grave. Although local police were given the names of fifteen people suspected of participating in the mob, no one was ever arrested or charged with the murders.

Finally, in January 1921, U.S. District Attorney Hooper Alexander of Atlanta declared in a statement that federal authorities were going to begin a statewide investigation to crack down on peonage. "Comparatively little effort is being made by the proper authorities to end these conditions. In a large proportion of the cases judicial processes are issued by magistrates that are used in the most shameless manner in the aid of crimes, and the attendant circumstances are such as should call for indictments for mal-practice. Cases have occurred in which there is the gravest reasons to fear that other officers of the law have been active participants in the gravest kind of wrongs. Things of which I speak run all the gamut from the meanest of petty cheating to deliberate and plotted murder. Ninety percent of our people would utterly deplore and condemn what is going on, but something more is demanded of civilized people and their government than mere sentiment. If the people of the state permit the continuance of what now prevails, sooner or later and in some way, we will suffer a dreadful retribution."[121]

A month later, after authorities showed up at a plantation in Jasper County, Georgia, owner John S. Williams and his three sons decided to destroy evidence of their enslaving of Blacks. With the help of Clyde Manning, a Black foreman, Williams and his sons ordered the murders of eleven African-American peons. In his confession, Manning told authorities, "I knocked four negroes in the head with an ax in one week and buried them in a pasture back of Mr. Johnny's (Williams) house. Why did I do it? Because the boss said he wanted to get rid of them negroes and that if I didn't make 'em disappear, he'd kill me. And I knew he meant what he said."[122]

Manning, a 26-year-old farm boss who had arrived at Williams' plantation at age 13, shortly after his father was murdered, confessed that another Black worker had helped kill the laborers. "Then, a little later Mr. Williams got uneasy about Charlie and made me get him. Me and Mr. Johnny took him to the river one night and pitched him off the bridge after we weighted him down. Charlie begged hard, but Mr. Johnny said: 'Let's throw him over and have it over with.'" All told, Manning said he helped Williams, a 54-year-old father of twelve, throw six Blacks into the river.[123]

"We took the other five to the river at night, after getting them out of their houses, and chained 'em down with rocks and threw 'em in," Manning confessed. "Yes, sir, they all cried and begged—and some of 'em asked to be knocked in the head before being thrown in, but Mr. Johnny wouldn't do it and wouldn't let me do it—we just threw them off the bridge and rode back to the plantation."[124]

Authorities found three bodies in the Yellow and South Rivers near Williams' plantation, five bodies in shallow graves, and three more in the Alcovy River. Manning testified that most of the workers who were killed had come to the plantation from cities such as Atlanta and Macon, after Williams's son, Huland, paid their fines and had them released from the blockade. "[T]hey brought the negroes to the farm and put 'em to work, and kept guards over 'em all the time so as not to let 'em get away or talk too much. I don't know whether they got any pay or not—I know Mr. Johnny paid me $20 a month and board."[125]

"Of course, mister, I'm sorry I knocked all them boys in the head and helped Mr. Johnny do away with them others, but there wasn't nothing else I could do—the boss told me If I didn't do as he said, I would be the next dead negro around there. I admits I have always been afraid of Mr. Williams. When he got ready to kill a negro, he would come to me and say, 'Clyde, I'm scared of that negro.' Then he would tell me what he wanted done, and being as I was working for him and couldn't get away myself, I had to go ahead and do it."[126]

A grand jury indicted Williams and Manning for three counts of murder. Williams blamed an adjoining farmer for the unsubstantiated allegations but admitted to bailing some Black workers out of jail, "just as other farmers" did. He said that he "paid them salaries." "There has been nothing illegal in such transactions of mine."[127]

Later, witnesses told authorities that Black workers had been killed on Williams's plantation since 1910. One was killed because he ran away twice, and a man and a wife were killed "because they were too old to do any more work." A witness said workers were locked up at night and had balls and chains fastened to their legs during the day. They were beaten and whipped when their work lagged. One Black worker said he was employed at the plantation for six years, for which he was paid one dollar.[128]

After the horrific details of the "Death Farm" were published in newspapers across the country, then-Georgia Governor Hugh M. Dorsey declared, "After some communities in Georgia have driven away their farm labor and their farm loans, they will have an opportunity to sit down and think over calmly whether it pays to deal justly with the negro."[129]

"The chief executive of the state and its thousands of better citizens are in accord that any traces of peonage must be stamped out," journalist Marion Kendrick wrote in the *Atlanta Constitution* shortly before the trial. "A blanket indictment of the state, in the opinion of its citizens, should not be made because there is a bad class existing within its borders."[130]

Vincent Hughes, then-head of the U.S. Justice Department's Bureau of Investigation (now known as the Federal Bureau of Investigation), told Kendrick that most peonage victims were "country negroes," and that the majority of complaints were from tenant farmers. In those cases, planters rented land to tenant farmers, or sharecroppers, and supplied them with necessities such as mules, cottonseed, tools, and fertilizer. The tenant farmer supplied the labor and would then receive about one-quarter to one-half of the crop—at least that is how the arrangement was supposed to work. In many instances, crops were unfairly divided or the tenant farmer didn't receive any payment for his work because of accrued debt.

During Williams's trial, his defense attorneys attempted to argue that the charges were a conspiracy by Dorsey, federal investigators, and urban liberals from Atlanta. On April 9, 1921, an all-White and all-male jury of farmers and small-town merchants in Covington, Georgia, did what was then considered inconceivable—they convicted Williams of murdering Lindsey Peterson, "an insignificant negro 'bought out' from a city prison and taken to work on his broad fields of cotton."[131] State Judge John B. Hutcheson sentenced Williams to life in prison, after the jury spared him from death. "We wrangled and wrangled so long," one of the jurors told reporters after the trial, "that I couldn't even guess how many ballots we took. The whole difference was about whether we ought to break his neck."[132]

More than a month later, an all-White jury convicted Manning of murder and sentenced him to life in prison. The state soon indicted three of Williams's sons, Huland, Leroy, and Marvin, for the murders of three Black laborers. Huland and Marvin Williams were fugitives for nearly six years; Leroy turned himself in after four years on the run.[133] Manning died of tuberculosis in 1927. John Williams died in an accident in prison in 1932.

It is beyond comprehension to me that the night before the jury in John Williams's trial reached a verdict, Williams's eldest son, Dr. Gus Williams, a hero in the battles of the Somme and Argonne Forest during World War I, told reporters, "I wish you all could have known papa and the rest of us before all this happened. Things might have looked different to you. We've always been a right happy family. And all the neighbors liked papa."[134]

CHAPTER EIGHT

WORKING FOR HALVES

IRCUMSTANCES REMAINED UNTENABLE EVEN FOR THOSE WHO managed to move up to the level of sharecropper in the years to come. When some children of Black farmers who grew up working on plantations were ultimately able to lift themselves up from that reality, they testified to the conditions and injustices they and their families experienced in writing.

One such person was David Jordan, a Democratic state senator from Mississippi who was raised on a plantation in The Delta during the Great Depression. The youngest of five children born to Black sharecroppers, David realized early in life that there was one thing he didn't want to do for long—labor in the fields.

"I was the weakest worker in the family when it came to picking cotton and it remained that way until the end of my cotton picking days," Jordan wrote in his 2014 book *David L. Jordan: From the Mississippi Cotton Field to the State Senate, a Memoir.* "I stayed in trouble throughout the years because I was frequently caught daydreaming in the field. I knew at an early age that I didn't want to spend the rest of my life doing something that was so menial and which negatively affected my sense of self-worth. I wanted to use my brain for something more than standing on my feet all day with the sizzling sun beaming down on my head."[135]

Picking cotton was the only thing Jordan's parents, Elizabeth and Cleveland Jordan, had ever known. Senator Jordan was born on April 3, 1933, on the Lawyer Whittington Plantation, just outside Greenwood in Leflore County, Mississippi. Jordan's mother nursed her children in the cotton fields. His brothers and sister received their first cotton bags around the age of three. At the end of each season, Jordan's father asked the overseer if he could have any of the worn-out bags, which he then used as bed sheets for his children.

"Laborers picked cotton that grew in long rows; we worked, like the slaves did in the antebellum period of the cotton culture, from sunrise to sunset," Jordan wrote.[136]

When Jordan was barely a year old, his family moved from the Lawyer Whittington Plantation to the Charles Whittington Plantation. The six-mile trip took almost eight hours with two mules pulling a covered wagon in cold rain. The plantations were among several owned by the family of U.S. Congressman William Madison Whittington, who represented the Mississippi Delta from 1925 to 1951.

According to Jordan's book, his family's new home had no electricity or indoor plumbing. Their drinking water came from a well. Jordan said his family earned eleven dollars for every bale of cotton, which typically meant thirty-three dollars in wages per week. However, they were paid for only half the bales they picked.

"I began to understand as I grew older how the system on the plantation actually worked," Jordan wrote. "We were considered share-croppers, and though the details sometimes differed, the sharecropping system was as follows. If the croppers picked thirty bales of cotton, then fifteen went to the plantation owner and fifteen to the sharecroppers. It was the sharecroppers' responsibility to pay the expenses of fertilizer, cultivation, seeds, and interest out of their fifteen bales. Needless to say, this wasn't a truly fair split."[137]

Nor was the split equitable when it came time to divide the fruits and vegetables Jordan's family grew in fields and gardens every summer. The plantation owner got half of that yield, too, even though he had done nothing to help produce it. "If we pulled ten loads of corn, then automatically half of the harvest belonged to the owner of the plantation, Mr. Whittington. There was always a set of eyes watching us to make sure that we were being fair when it came to distributing the corn. It didn't matter that it was our hard work that pulled the corn. We used a wagon to be sure that the corn got delivered to the barn, where Mr. Whittington would wait for his half. This was just the way things were and it didn't appear that anything was going to change anytime soon."[138]

The plantation owner didn't always pay Jordan's father in cash; he received a coupon book that could be used to purchase goods in the plantation store. The family's lean cupboard consisted of staples such as canned pork and beans, oil, sausage, molasses, and salmon. There were two cows that supplied the family with milk, plus whatever sweet potatoes, greens, and corn they could grow. "It always seemed like our food supplies were barely enough," Jordan wrote, "but somehow they proved sufficient to keep us going."[139]

Jordan's father tried to save enough money each year to put a new pair of shoes on his children's feet. They had to last until the end of the next growing season, even if they were worn in the cotton fields for countless hours almost every summer day. Back then, the school year for Blacks ran from December to April to allow children to work in the fields with their parents.

Jordan recalled his father telling him about an incident in which he confronted the plantation's "boss man" about paying him in cash instead of coupons for groceries. Jordan's father knew it would have been cheaper to buy food at another store in town. Jordan and three other Black men had agreed to approach the owner on a Saturday morning. Jordan's father showed up at the store; the other men didn't.

"Of course, Poppa told us, when it was time to confront the boss with the request he was standing alone," Jordan wrote. "He said that he never forgot the look on Mr. Whittington's face when he confronted him on that Saturday morning. Mr. Whittington said to my poppa,

'Cleveland, if you weren't such a good nigga, I would kill you! Those other niggas came here and got their groceries last night, and told me of your plot! So, you know the only thing that is saving you is that you're a good working nigga.'"[140]

Across the reconstructed South, sharecropping became another means for White landowners to continue to maintain their dominance, both financially and socially, over newly freed African-American slaves, who greatly outnumbered them. While White landowners preferred gang-style labor, similar to what was employed during slavery before the Civil War, most freedmen refused to return to plantations under those abhorrent conditions. They wanted the freedom to choose where they worked and for whom they worked, while maintaining the dream of one day owning land.

In essence, sharecroppers were one step up the plantation ladder from day laborers, peons, and convict laborers. Sharecroppers, or tenant farmers, leased small homesteads, ranging from ten to thirty acres, depending on the number of hands in the households, including wives and children. Their profits were largely determined by the landowners' honesty and, even more so, Mother Nature. A crop could be wiped out by drought, floods, disease, and, eventually, the boll weevil.

"Although nominally more independent than day laborers, these tenants nonetheless met with close supervision from plantation managers, who determined when to plant and harvest, and deducted any additional services, such as plowing, dusting, or ginning, from the croppers' accounts. At the end of the season, croppers, as true share-tenants, received anywhere from a quarter to half the value of the harvested cotton and cottonseed (hence, the phrases 'working on quarters' or 'working on halves'). The landlord, however, retained control of the crop's marketing as well as the settlement of accounts. This final reckoning of the plantation books rarely favored the cropper, who often cleared only $50 to $150 in a good season, and dipped further into debt during a bad one."[141]

During the late nineteenth and early twentieth century, the vast majority of African-American and poor White farmers were landless. They were primarily operating as tenant farmers on White plantations like the ones Senator Jordan described. But soon the demographics of tenant farming began to change. In 1880, only a third of farmers in Louisiana were sharecroppers, but by 1910, the number had increased to about 55 percent.[142] Due to the severe worldwide economic distress caused by the Great Depression, more and more White farmers had to become sharecroppers after their plantations and farms were foreclosed. By 1930 there were 1,831,470 tenant farmers in the South. Just five years later, almost half of White farmers and 77 percent of Black farmers in the U.S. were landless.[143] In 1940, there were only 58,000 more Black than White sharecroppers in the Southern plantation states of South Carolina, Georgia, Alabama, Mississippi, Louisiana, and Arkansas.[144]

Most sharecroppers had agreements with landowners similar to the one Jordan's family had in Mississippi. For example, the land where Clemson University is located in Clemson, South Carolina, was once a plantation called Fort Hill, which was owned by the family of the former U.S. vice president and senator John C. Calhoun. The Special Collections and Archives at Clemson University Libraries contain actual articles of agreement between freedmen and women and Thomas Green Clemson, the university's namesake, thus contributing to a record of how some of these arrangements worked.

Clemson was born in Philadelphia and later married into the slave-holding Calhoun family. He was a U.S. ambassador to Belgium from 1844 to 1852. After the Civil War broke out, he enlisted in the Confederacy in 1863. As a mining engineer, he was placed in charge of nitrate mines in Arkansas and Texas, which were used to produce explosives. When the Civil War ended, he was paroled in 1865 and granted a pardon by President Andrew Johnson about a year later.[145]

From 1868 to 1871, following the death of his mother-in-law, Floride Calhoun, Clemson signed contracts with freedmen and women who worked at Fort Hill. Clemson's contracts included ten to fifteen articles of agreement, stipulating, for example, that farmers "not keep fire arms or deadly weapons," that there be "no arduous spirits," and that they "not ...invite visitors, nor leave the premises during work hours without ...written consent."[146] According to research conducted by Rhondda Robinson Thomas, a literature professor at Clemson University, at least

129 enslaved people worked for the Calhoun and Clemson families at Fort Hill. Many of them remained as indentured servants or sharecroppers after the Thirteenth Amendment freed them.[147]

In most instances, articles of agreement with sharecroppers were grossly one-sided toward landowners. For instance, Clemson's third article in an 1868 agreement docked sharecroppers pay for absences, even if they were sick: "For every day's labor lost by absence, refusal or neglect to perform the daily task, or labor said servants shall forfeit fifty cents. If absent voluntarily, or without authority, or without leave two dollars a day; if absent more than one day without leave to be subject to dismissal from the plantation [and] forfeiture of share in crop. The dependents or families of such laborer or laborers shall immediately vacate their houses within the space of three days [and] quit the plantation. All such fines, [and] forfeitures shall inure to the [benefit] of the employer [and] employees in proportion to their relative shares."[148]

Clemson's articles of agreement also charged sharecroppers with taking care of tools and equipment they were given to farm, as well as the livestock they used to plow. "Said Freed-men [and] women agree to take good care of all utensils, tools, and implements committed to their charge [and] to pay for same if injured or destroyed, also to feed [and] curry, [and] give attention to all stock put under their charge, to be kind [and] gentle to all work animals under their charge: [and] to pay for any injury which they may sustain while in their hands through their carelessness or neglect, [and] forfeitures here in specified will be subject to the decision of the authorities having proper jurisdiction of the same."[149]

In the clause regarding provisions, Clemson agreed to supply housing, feed for animals, and other amenities on the plantation with certain conditions. "The said employer agrees to treat his employees with justice [and] kindness; to furnish each family with quarters on the plantation, [and] the privilege of getting fire wood from some portion of the premises to be indicated by the employer or his agent, [and] to devide the crop with them in the following manner, [and] proportions to wit: to the employees one third of the fodder [cereal crops like corn and wheat], cotton, potatoes, peas, [and] oats, they paying back their proportion of seed gathered and prepared for market or its market value at the end of the year. And the said T.G. Clemson agrees to furnish the usual bread rations to be accounted for at the market price out of their share of the crop."[150]

Lastly, the agreement specified that the sharecroppers were expected to work from sunrise until dark and were given one hour or more for meals, depending on the season of the year. "The time for going to work [and] recall will be made known by sound of horn [and] so punctually observed," the contract concluded.

As part of his last will following his death from pneumonia in 1888, Clemson left 814 acres of land and more than $80,000 in other assets to the state of South Carolina to establish an agricultural college at the Fort Hill estate.[151] The Clemson Agricultural College of South Carolina was established in 1889.

Among other testaments to conditions in the South during the early twentieth century was that of William Gordon. Gordon's family worked as sharecroppers in Mississippi and Arkansas in the 1920s and 1930s. He recalled a White farm boss riding horseback with a gun on his hip, as he worked in cotton fields at a plantation in Ruleville, Mississippi.

"He was the overseer and you never argued with him about anything," Gordon said. "He just said this and you did it. We would be in the fields chopping [with] my mother and others .... We would be working along in the fields and this man would ride up on his horse. This was not only true in our case but true for just about everybody there."[152]

One day, when Gordon was about eight years old, he was walking to a school for Blacks that was located in a rural church. That's when he and some of the other children encountered a body draped in a white sheet lying on the ground.

"[H]is feet were protruding, we could see that," Gordon said. "That frightened the heck out of us and we ran all the way to school which was about another mile. When we got there the teacher told us that this was a man who was killed because he had some words with the overseer. Nobody ever investigated the killing."

On another day, Gordon's stepfather had a confrontation with the overseer and then vanished for two or three weeks. A man from a neighboring farm knocked on their door. The neighbor had heard from his stepfather. Three nights later, his stepfather showed up with a wagon.

"[T]hat was pretty typical of the black sharecroppers in those days, you just went away and then send for your family later," Gordon said.

Gordon and his family took a train to Helena, Arkansas, and they eventually settled in a town called Marked Tree, Arkansas, northwest of Memphis. The overseer at that farm was more accommodating than the former one.

"He worked in the fields with everybody else," Gordon said.

The overseer even encouraged Gordon and his siblings to attend a nearby school for Blacks.

"Whenever the crops were laid and there was a break in the spring or summer, we could always go to school," Gordon said. "He was very liberal in that respect. He had three kids himself, a daughter and two sons. They went into Marked Tree to school. He used to say, 'Learning is good for you, so go to school. I send my kids to school, so you go.' We went to school and we had no problem there."

Gordon's landowner was the exception to the rule in the Deep South. Ed Brown, a sharecropper from Abbeville, Georgia, worked for White landowners during the 1920s and 1930s. After the introduction of the tractor and other machinery dramatically reduced the need for farm laborers, Brown and his wife became domestic servants for a White family in Atlanta and then New York. One of the family's daughters, Jane Maguire, became interested in his tales of working as a Black farm-hand. Brown was illiterate, but Jane persuaded him to let her help him share his experiences. She documented his life in the 1976 book *On Shares: Ed Brown's Story.*

Brown started picking cotton when he was eight years old. His stepfather worked him especially hard, he said, because he and his sister Rose were the children of a White man his mother had cooked for. In 1929, after Brown was grown and married, he went to work on shares for a White farmer named Leslie Prince, who promised to pay him ten dollars per month. Until the cotton crop was picked and baled, Prince paid him an advance, at fifteen percent interest, but not all was in cash.

Brown told Maguire that the landowner made sure he purchased as much meat, syrup, and other goods as he could from his smokehouse to keep his pay down. "Then, on shares, the boss furnish you with the land, mule, seeds, tools, and one half of the fertilizer. I was to put out the other half of the fertilizer and all of the labor."[153]

One day, according to Ed, he picked one hundred and thirty-five pounds of cotton. At the end of the season, he turned in seven bales of cotton and two horse wagons full of corn. Prince claimed that still wasn't enough to cover his sixty-dollar advance.

"But hard work didn't get me nowhere," Brown told Maguire. "Mr. Prince wouldn't show me the papers the gin and the warehouse give him, so I didn't know what the crop had brung and what my share should be. He took his share and all of mine and claim I owe him twenty-four dollars in addition .... He put the corn in the crib without weighin it. Velvet beans was bringin a dollar a hundred pounds, and he took all of them. And all the sweet potatoes."[154]

That wasn't all that the White farmer wanted either. He also wanted Ed's dairy cow.

"Me and my wife had brung the cow and the calf I swapped for my Model T Ford with us from the Addison place. We brung two hogs, and I had give Mr. Prince one to let me fatten the other in the peanut field. He took both of them."[155]

When Ed confronted the farmer on his porch later that day, Prince told his son to get his knife. That night, Prince showed up at Ed's house and asked him to discuss the problem in a pitch-black cotton field.

"I seed there wasn't no use talkin. If it had been fair as a lily and he'd said it was rainin and I'd said no, he'd said I was disputin his word. And if you had met him, you'd a thought he was the best man in the world .... He'd got to the table every mornin and say a long prayer over it, and then he'd come right out of that house and take every bit of bread out of your mouth. And he'd raise more sand than forty lawyers."[156]

If it weren't for a unique public works program, some other sharecroppers' stories might never have been told. In response to the Great Depression, Congress passed the Emergency Relief Appropriation Act of 1935, which was designed to get 11.3 million unemployed Americans back to work. One of programs it funded was the Federal Writers' Project, which provided employment for writers, teachers, historians, and others who had lost their jobs. Writers from around the country interviewed former slaves and sharecroppers to document more than two thousand first-person accounts, which are now stored at the Library of Congress.

Jim Parker, a 62-year-old tenant farmer, was interviewed by one of the writers on June 7, 1939. At the time of the interview, he had been sharecropping for twenty-two years. He was ready to quit, but said he owed the landowner money on the previous year's crop. "I ain't doin' what I want to do," he said. "The only reason I took another crop with [the landowner] this year was cause I owed him some money on last year's account, and I don't want to leave a man owin' him. What I want wus'n anything in this world is a home and a little farm that's mine."[157]

Jim's father, Zebedee Parker, was a former slave and a sharecropper in Virginia, so this was a life Jim knew well. For a time Jim worked "shovelin' dirt and keepin' up with railroad ties" before taking a job at a sawmill for ten years, earning seventy-five cents to a dollar per day. Once he was married and had children, he returned to sharecropping, making about two hundred to one thousand dollars a year, after paying for whatever rations he took from the plantation owner's store.

Jim Parker said he tried twice to operate his own farm but failed. After seven years of tenant farming, he bought forty-three acres near Garysburg, North Carolina, about one hundred miles southwest of Virginia Beach. He negotiated a purchase price of $3,800 for the land, making a down payment of one thousand dollars. The first year, he made a payment of five hundred dollars. When his crops went south the next year, he was almost two hundred dollars in the hole. He couldn't make the mortgage payment, so he lost the land—and the $1,500 he had already paid.

Parker said he returned to sharecropping. By then, he and his wife had thirteen children to feed. The landowner paid them fifty dollars per month to live on, and he worked a "five-horse crop." There wasn't much disposable income at the end of the year, but after ten years Parker had saved enough to buy a horse from the landowner.

"That was the cause of our first misunderstandin'," Parker said. "Mr. Tommie charged the ho'se against my account that year, claimin' I didn't pay him, when I knowed I had. I lost it."

A second disagreement involved the landowner charging Parker for fertilizer he hadn't used. "There was gettin' to be too much difference in our books," he said. "So after ten years I decided it was time to move on to another place."

Parker tried to buy his own place for a second time. The Land Bank in Raleigh, North Carolina, permitted him to buy a homestead for $4,500 and "pay for it along as I was able." He was never able to make a payment and lost that farm too.

"It looks like I ought to have somethin' to show for the money I've made," Parker said, while being interviewed by Bernice Kelly Harris. "The highest that ever come in one year's work was $1,000, and the least was $190 less than nothin'. It's taken it all. I invested $1,500 in a farm and lost it, paid $300 out for my wife's operation, bought a ho'se and one car …fed fifteen chil'en, myself, and wife, and give 'em a few clothes. Today I don't have a cent I can call my own.…We don't have nothin' to show for hard work but what little goes on the table."

Looking back on his life, Parker wished he had done something other than sharecropping.

"Livin' on another man's land, takin' his orders about a investment that's half ours, subject to get movin' orders any time, and havin' to accept a settlement we know ain't right, havin' nothin' to look forward to but meat and bread and dissatisfaction—no, I wouldn't sharecrop if I didn't have to."

After nearly a half-century of plowing another man's dirt, Parker still dreamed of owning his own farm—once he paid off the one hundred and fifty dollars he owed his landlord.

"As I look back on my sixty-two years, I don't see hardly how I could done no better'n I have," Parker said. "My daddy, after freedom, spent his life sharecroppin', movin' round from place to place, and died not ownin' a foot o' ground. I aimed to do better'n that, but looks like I ain't made much improvements on his record. He eat and wore clothes; that's about where I am now."

CHAPTER NINE

NEW DEAL

W HEN FRANKLIN DELANO ROOSEVELT ASSUMED THE U.S. PRESI-
dency on March 4, 1933, nearly a quarter of America's workforce
were unemployed. During the previous four years, about nine thousand banks, which held the savings of more than 27 million families, had
failed, and thousands more were in danger of going under. Every day,
thousands of families were losing their homes. Additionally, there were
twenty thousand farm foreclosures every month. More than one million
people were homeless.

Conditions were so bleak in rural America that the journalist
Lorena Hickok, a close friend of First Lady Eleanor Roosevelt, would
famously note after traveling through Georgia that she had seen "half-
starved Whites and Blacks struggle in competition for less to eat than
my dog gets at home, for the privilege of living in huts that are infinitely
less comfortable than his kennel."[158]

America's economy and future had never seemed so dire. By the end of Roosevelt's second day in the White House, he ordered every bank in America to close for a national "bank holiday"—a measure intended to halt the hoarding of currency and gold. Banks remained closed for more than a week after that, as the president and his advisers sorted through how to rescue the economy.

Roosevelt's solution was a "new deal for the American people" centered on "relief, recovery, and reform." The Federal Emergency Relief Administration would provide cash payments to the unemployed, and the Civilian Conservation Corps would put 300,000 young men back to work building bridges and roads, planting trees, and cleaning parks and beaches. The Public Works Administration would spend more than $3.3 billion with private companies to construct airports, bridges, dams, post offices, hospitals, and other government buildings.

During Roosevelt's "first 100 days," agricultural advocates pushed for equally impactful measures to rescue the American farmer. Fortunately for them, Roosevelt believed the struggles of agriculture were at the core of the Great Depression. To save farmers, FDR signed the Agricultural Adjustment Act (AAA) in May 1933. Roosevelt's agricultural bill had two main objectives: financially assisting poor farmers and raising the price of farm goods, which were being threatened by overproduction, natural disasters, and other market factors such as foreign tariffs and, in the case of cotton, the emergence of new and competing fabrics.

The livelihood of American farmers was already in danger before the stock market crash of 1929. Farmers across the country were devastated by declining demand and prices, blight, drought, soil erosion, and other negative factors. It's helpful to look at each of these individually.

During World War I, American farmers had increased production dramatically to meet the needs of the global market. By 1920, after the war ended, demand and farm income fell sharply. Farmers were making less than half of what they had earned only a few years before.

A survey of 60,000 farmers in the early 1920s revealed that 4 percent had lost their property to bankruptcy or foreclosure; 4.5 percent had voluntarily deeded their farms to creditors; and 15 percent were on the verge of bankruptcy.[159] By 1929, total farm debt stood at $9.8 billion.[160]

There were myriad other reasons for the collapse of American agriculture. Among them was the boll weevil, a Central American insect that feeds on cotton buds and flowers. It first entered the U.S. from Mexico in 1892 near Brownsville, Texas.[161] From there, it spread to cover 600,000 square miles in three decades and reaching all cotton-producing areas of the U.S. by the 1920s. The menacing pest ravaged the cotton industry and led to the destruction of millions of acres of cotton fields. After it was introduced in Georgia, the state's cotton yield decreased from 5.2 million acres in 1914 to only 2.6 million in 1923.[162] And in Alabama, it caused production to fall in 1916 from 155 pounds per acre to 95 pounds per acre.[163] At the same time as boll weevils were wreaking havoc on our farmlands, the demand for cotton fell, causing prices across the country to decrease from 28.8 cents per pound to 17.98 cents per pound between 1918 and 1928.[164] In response, many Southern farmers replaced cotton with cash crops such as corn, which depleted the soil of nutrients and led, in turn, to widespread erosion.

In the Great Plains, the Dust Bowl of the 1930s all but wiped out farming in parts of Colorado, Kansas, New Mexico, Oklahoma, and Texas. The thick native grasslands there had been used mostly for livestock grazing until World War I, when millions of acres were converted to wheat fields during a period known as the "Great Plow-Up." This expansion of farmland in addition to poor land management practices increased the region's vulnerability to drought.

Things only got worse when crop prices fell. Emboldened by the advancement of tractors and other equipment, farmers across the Great Plains decided to put more land into production hoping they could recoup the difference in income through volume. The new tractors, plows, and listers allowed them to work the larger farms, but it also meant that they needed to produce more wheat to pay for this equipment, which was often purchased on credit. Many farmers abandoned soil conservation practices to cut costs. Overproduction, in turn, sent wheat prices spiraling downward. Oklahoma wheat farmers, who had yielded $1.2 million in 1931 yielded only a paltry $7,000 in 1933. North Dakota farmers spent 77 cents to produce a bushel of wheat in 1932 whereas they were only paid 30 cents per bushel when they sold it.[165] That was only the beginning of their struggles.

According to the National Drought Mitigation Center at the University of Nebraska, there were at least four distinct droughts in the Great Plains from 1930 to 1940, and they occurred right on top of one another. Collectively, they led to the worst man-made disaster on record. Windstorms stripped topsoil from more than one hundred million acres of farmland and sent dust storms as far away as the East Coast.

An estimated 3.5 million people fled the Great Plains to look for employment between 1930 and 1940, many of them settling in California, where they worked as migrant farmers.[166] By 1937, according to a Works Progress Administration bulletin, about 21 percent of rural families in the Great Plains were receiving some form of federal assistance. "However, even with government help, many farmers could not maintain their operations and were forced to leave their land. Some voluntarily deeded their farms to creditors, others faced foreclosure by banks, and still others had to leave temporarily to search for work to provide for their families. In fact, at the peak of farm transfers in 1933–34, nearly 1 in 10 farms changed possession, with half of those being involuntary (from a combination of the depression and drought)."[167]

The effects were being felt nationwide. Ed Brown, the Georgia sharecropper whom the author Jane Maguire wrote about in her book *On Shares: Ed Brown's Story*, described to her what life was like for farmers during "panic time."

"Durin the worst of the panic people was walkin to and fro, up and down the highway," Brown told Maguire. "Men would come into the settlement and go from house to house beggin for somethin, anythin to do. The white people could get a yard cut for thirty cents and hedges clipped for twenty-five cents. In 1930 I sold my cotton for five cents a pound. My share of that was two and a half cents. A man who didn't have no regular way of gettin food had to steal or starve."[168]

The evolution of the farm tractor made matters even worse for day laborers, tenant farmers, and sharecroppers. In 1903, Charles W. Hart and Charles H. Parr of Charles City, Iowa, built the first American tractor using a two-cylinder gasoline engine. The Hart Parr Company first coined the word "tractor" to describe their self-propelled traction engines. Between 1916 to 1922, there were more than one hundred companies building tractors in the U.S. John Deere, Allis-Chalmers, Ford, and International Harvester manufactured lightweight, all-purpose tractors, which allowed farmers to plant and cultivate three rows at once, eliminating the need for mules and laborers to lead them. By 1932, more than one million lightweight tractors had been sold in the U.S.[169]

"Just about the time of the panic the tractor come in strong," Brown told Maguire. "At first it didn't have rubber tires, just cleats that would catch in the ground. The driver would only work in the middle of the field, and men with mules went in the corners and along the fences, where you couldn't turn a tractor around. In just a few years the tractor improved so much it put the mule out of business. The landowner was quick to take a likin to the tractor. With it he would have no people to feed, no doctors' bills or houses to repair, and no mules to feed. He could buy fertilizer with the money he used to pay hands."[170]

According to Brown, "Men started walking the roads lookin for a farm, for a dry place to sleep, and a place to raise somethin to eat. Mr. So and So, they'd tell me, has got a tractor and I got to move. Some would walk weeks lookin for a farm."[171]

The tractor and other farm improvements such as hybrid seeds, commercial fertilizers, and weed killers drove tens of thousands of Black sharecroppers, tenant farmers, and day laborers to larger cities looking for work, contributing to the country's historic unemployment rates.

In what was either an unintended consequence or outright racial discrimination, the Agricultural Adjustment Act of 1933 put Black farmers even more at risk. The AAA essentially paid farmers, through subsidies, to reduce their crops in an effort to curtail overproduction, which would stabilize the markets. The subsidies were paid through a federal excise tax imposed on companies that processed farm products. In the beginning, the AAA established domestic allotments for seven basic farm products—wheat, cotton, corn, tobacco, rice, hogs, and milk and its products. More than half of the country's farmers voluntarily signed allotment contracts, removing more than thirty million acres from production in exchange for $1.1 billion in subsidies.[172]

Local newspapers and AAA offices around the country aggressively encouraged farmers to join the federal program. A newspaper in Alexandria, Louisiana, called the federal program "the greatest effort that has ever been attempted to aid the cotton producers of this parish and the entire South in lifting themselves out of their present economic condition."

"Each producer has the opportunity in the 1934-1935 cotton program to do the things which every informed and reasonable thinking farmer agrees ought to be done and get pay for doing it. There are many farmers in this parish who did not produce sufficient food and feed crops to maintain their farming operations in the past. They have the opportunity of renting from 35 percent to 45 percent of their average cotton acreage that has been planted in cotton from 1928 to 1932, inclusive, to the government and still have these rented acres to grow the crops they need to maintain their farm through the year."

The federal cotton program, according to the report, would "go a long way in solving the present cotton surplus problem and bring the cotton belt cash payments of approximately $125,000,000 in addition securing for them a better price for cotton."[173]

Since many farmers had already planted crops by the time the AAA took effect, they simply plowed up their fields. In Arkansas, for example, farmers were told to reduce their cotton production by more than one million acres. They had planted more than three million acres of cotton in 1931.[174] Millions of cows, hogs, sheep, and other livestock were butchered to qualify for government payments. This destruction came at a time when millions of Americans were out of work and struggling to eat because of the Great Depression. Facing mounting criticism, Congress created the Commodity Credit Corporation to distribute surplus food, including butter, cheese, flour, and meat, to the unemployed. Over the first three years of the Agricultural Adjustment Act, corn, cotton, and wheat prices doubled. In 1932, the average annual income in the U.S. was $385; farmers earned only $115 per year. Three years later, because of the federal programs, farmers' income had increased to $255.[175]

Many of the banks that failed were located in rural areas and had provided farmers with much-needed loans to cover crop production costs. Congress passed the Farm Credit Act in 1933 to refinance mortgages and improve federal lending to farmers to plant their crops. The Farm Credit Administration sought to consolidate and streamline federal loans and mortgages to farmers. Congress passed legislation to delay farm foreclosures to allow farmers to remain on their land.

On January 6, 1936, the U.S. Supreme Court ruled that key provisions of the Agricultural Adjustment Act were unconstitutional and that states, and not the federal government, should control agriculture. A new federal agricultural act was enacted in 1938 that remedied the problems highlighted by the Supreme Court and added crop insurance.

Yet the New Deal programs only exacerbated the plight of the Black farmer in the South. By 1930, of the more than 4.8 million Blacks employed in the U.S., more than two million worked in agriculture. More than three-fourths of those who worked on farms were tenant farmers and almost one-half of those were sharecroppers, who were at the bottom rung of the agriculture food chain.[176] The mostly White landowners who received the federal government payments to take their land out of production accounted for only about one-fourth of the people engaged in cotton farming in the South. According to the 1930 U.S. Census, there were 936,896 White tenant farmers and 670,665 Black tenant families working on farms in the ten cotton-producing states.[177]

When landowners agreed to take their land out of cultivation for subsidy checks from the federal government, they eliminated the need for tenant farmers and sharecroppers, who were most often working the least productive sections of land.

Newspaper reports in early 1934 suggested that farm relief would reach $350 million to help relocate 600,000 displaced families, "who are victims of the farm depression and of the struggle to pull agriculture out of the depression mire. Already thousands of these families are on the move in the South. Other thousands are digging in to wait for the helping hand from Washington to give them a new start in life. . . .Most are caught by plans to cut by 50,000,000 acres the amount of land planted to crops. Many are former tenants. Others in the north are farm laborers. The greater number proportionately are concentrated in the cotton-growing states of the south.

Now they are cut loose, dependent upon the generosity of landlords, and upon the forethought of Uncle Sam."[178]

According to the report, 300,000 families were estimated to have lived on those 15 million acres of former cotton fields that would become idle. As University of Southern Mississippi history professor Charles C. Bolton noted in 2004, "Landowners bought tractors to break the land, bought newly developed cotton harvesters to pick their crops, and bought pesticides to rid their fields of weeds (previously 'chopped out' by tenants and sharecroppers). In the process, Mississippi's system of farm tenancy and sharecropping quickly came to an end."[179]

White farmers and landlords were under increasing pressure to terminate contracts with their tenant farmers and sharecroppers. With as much as 40 percent of a landowner's land being unused, his expenses would remain the same if he kept the same number of tenants. "If he evicted tenants he would not have to support them, he would not have to split government benefit money with them, and he could use the rented acres for his own purposes. AAA's rental checks, coming early in the season as they did, gave him money with which to hire day workers or wage hands to cultivate and harvest the crop. Such workers had no rights under the contract, so with them the landlord could return to the relation he wanted with his labor, one in which the government did not interfere. Only those landlords who sincerely wished to comply with their contract, who feared to violate it, or who felt a paternalistic responsibility toward their tenants, resisted the temptation to evict. Fortunately, they were in the vast majority."[180]

However, the late historian David Eugene Conrad found that cotton plantation owners also lowered the status of tenants from share-tenants to croppers or from croppers to day workers. "The motivations for land-lords to downgrade their tenants were about the same for evictions," Conrad wrote. "They would not have to split rental payments or tax exemptions with share-tenants-made-croppers nor would they have to provide, 'furnish' or divide parity payments with croppers who had been forced to become day workers."[181] The AAA said it wouldn't grant contracts to any farmers who had side agreements with their tenants, but there was little for the White landlords to lose.

"Despite the efforts of AAA to prevent it," Conrad wrote, "there were many instances where the status of tenants was lowered. The timing of benefit payments had something to do with it. By the end of spring, 1934, every landlord had received half of his rental payment, and by the end of summer the other half. All that remained then was the parity payment, which amounted to only about 22 percent of the total benefits. Thus, before the crop was harvested the landlord had received 78 percent of what the government intended to pay him. He would violate the contract any way he wanted to and still lose only the remaining 22 percent."[182]

For whatever reason, there were inadequate safeguards in place to protect the most vulnerable tenant farmers, sharecroppers, and other non-land-owning farmers when it came to issuing payments for acreage reductions as part of the agriculture recovery plan. While the contracts encouraged landowners to reduce the acreage of tenants and not take all of the rented land away, the condition was hardly enforced.

Calvin B. Hoover, a noted professor of economics at Duke University, was asked to examine the problems facing sharecroppers and tenant farmers by U.S. Secretary of Agriculture Henry A. Wallace. Hoover found that "various undesirable effects and instances of hardships to individuals have occurred in connection with the cotton acreage reduction program. In some cases these were due to the nature of the cotton contract itself, sometimes to its misinterpretation and sometimes to its violation."[183]

Hoover found that under the program, tenant farmers did not receive the full amount specified by the contracts, and that landowners were motivated to reduce the number of tenant farmers, even though the landlord had been warned "in good faith to bring about the reduction of acreage ... in such manner as to cause the least possible amount of labor, economic and social disturbance."

In most cases, Hoover discovered that landlords were allowed to sign the 1933 plow-up contracts for themselves and their tenants after receiving permission from the tenant farmers and sharecroppers. The government issued checks to the landowner and tenants, unless the tenants waived their rights.

"In practice, the matter often worked out quite differently," Hoover concluded. "In numbers of cases landlords did not obtain the consent of their tenants before signing the contract. They simply made no mention of having tenants who had an interest in the crops. Consequently, checks for benefit payments were often made out in the names of the landlord alone. He was thus given the opportunity to make any kind of settlement with his tenants that he wished. This situation arose largely due to the failure of the contract to recognize the existence of separate landlord and tenant interests."

With regard to federal loans for seed, fertilizer, and feed, the federal government found that White landowners were also taking advantage of Black tenants.

"In a few black-belt areas tenants got and spent the loans made to them; they bought their feed, seed, and fertilizer at cash prices and accordingly had relatively smaller debts in the fall. The planters, however, usually got control of their tenants' checks through an oral agreement between the landlord and the tenants. As a matter of fact, the landlord virtually forces the tenant to deliver the check to him; the landlord explains to the tenant that he will not waive his rent to the Government—one of the requirements for the loan—unless the tenant agrees to bring the check to him when it comes....In some instances, the planter has taken the money and deposited it to his own account, issuing cash back to the tenant as he thought the tenant needed it. The planter usually charges 8 to 10 percent interest. Thus, the tenant pays double interest—6 percent to the Government for the money and an additional 8 to 10 percent to the planter for keeping it for him."[184]

Another discriminatory aspect of the New Deal was the Federal Emergency Relief Act (FERA), which was designed to provide financial relief to state and local governments, which were being overwhelmed by the collapse of tax revenues and increasing costs of emergency relief to the unemployed. During a two-year period from 1933 to 1935, FERA provided more than $3 billion in aid to states, which assisted more than 20 million citizens, or about 16 percent of the U.S. population.[185]

Abril Castro and Zoe Willingham, researchers at the Center for American Progress, noted that Blacks were once again slighted when it came to receiving FERA funds during the Great Depression.

"In 1934, in Georgia's Greene and Macon counties, blacks were in greater need of assistance from the Federal Emergency Relief Administration but received less aid than whites," Castro and Willingham wrote. "In Greene County, blacks received 20 percent less direct relief than whites, even though the average rural white family earned twice as much as a black family. In Macon County, whites received double the amount of direct relief as blacks, even though the average income of a white family was almost triple that of a black family. The number of black farmers in the South decreased 8 percent from 1930 to 1935, while the number of white farmers increased by 11 percent."[186]

By passing the New Deal, the researchers noted, "government workers and actions helped maintain the pre-Civil War social hierarchy of the South."

CHAPTER TEN

REIGN OF TERROR

T HE TIME TO BAND TOGETHER TO ENACT CHANGE HAD FINALLY come.

As hundreds of onlookers grew impatient during a rally of the Southern Tenant Farmers' Union in Marked Tree, Arkansas, on January 15, 1935, Ward Rodgers, a 24-year-old graduate of Vanderbilt University, took the stage to address the crowd.

Only the day before, Rodgers, an educational worker for the Federal Emergency Relief Administration, had been warned by a school superintendent to leave town "or he might be found dead some morning."[187] When Rodgers asked if the order to leave came from the Ku Klux Klan, the superintendent purportedly told him to call it whatever he wanted.

"Well, that is a game two can play," Rodgers shouted to the crowd. "If necessary, I could lead the sharecroppers to lynch every planter in Poinsett County!"[188]

According to historian David Conrad, Black and White sharecroppers and tenant farmers alike cheered wildly and threw their hats in the air. Some shouted, "Let's go get 'em!" Rodgers was promptly arrested and jailed on charges of inciting a mob, anarchy, and conspiracy against the state. He was hastily tried and convicted of anarchy. He was sentenced to six months in prison and fined five hundred dollars.[189]

Rodgers and other White socialists had helped organize the Southern Tenant Farmers' Union (STFU) in the summer of 1934. The movement was in response to the actions of a local planter named Hiram Norcross, who had evicted twenty-three families from his farm earlier that spring as a result of the Agriculture Adjustment Act (AAA).

Fairview Farms, a 4,500-acre plantation near Tyronza, Arkansas, was originally operated by Hiram's father, who was killed when the horse he was riding threw him and broke his neck. Hiram, who was an attorney in Kansas City, leased part of his Fairview land, but then foreclosed on the buyers when the cotton market collapsed.

"When he did [that], he was strictly business," said Clay East, who helped organize the Arkansas tenant farmers and sharecroppers. "He drew up a contract for all of the sharecroppers and took an account of everything he let them have to work the land with. He didn't allow 'em to have a cow or chickens or anything."[190]

According to Conrad, Norcross was determined to turn a profit from his plantation, and the easiest means to do it was by evicting poor families.

He also squeezed every penny from those remaining. "Ordinarily, the planters in Arkansas allowed their sharecroppers credit at the commissary on a basis of one dollar a month for each acre farmed," Conrad wrote. "Norcross had his plantation surveyed and found that his commissary was allowing more credit than the plantation had acres. On other plantations it was custom to grant additional credit to croppers with large families, but Norcross decided to end that practice at Fairview."[191]

In light of these actions, seven Black and eleven White farmers met at the nearby Sunnyside School in July 1934. During this meeting, the men debated whether their new union should be integrated—and not separated by race—since Black and White tenant farmers shared the same longtime struggles with planters.

Isaac "Ike" Shaw, an elderly Black sharecropper, raised his voice. Fifteen years earlier, Shaw had survived the Elaine Massacre. It was on September 30, 1919 in Elaine, Arkansas, that several Black sharecroppers, who had formed the Progressive Farmers and Household Union of America (PFHUA), met with a prominent White attorney to talk about unfair wages.

Around 11 o'clock that night, a group of White men fired into the church where the Black farmers were meeting. Someone inside fired back, killing a White man. Literature that was later confiscated from the meeting indicated that the union had offices in Washington, D.C., and Winchester, Arkansas. White citizens feared that the Black farmers were leading an organized "insurrection." After Arkansas Governor Charles Hillman Brough was called, he ordered five hundred troops from nearby Camp Pike to be sent to Elaine.

According to one published report, the soldiers formed a perimeter around a densely wooded tract of land, where "150 heavily armed negroes, leaders of their race in riots which resulted in 12 more deaths in this vicinity during the last 24 hours," were hiding. "The troops were all under orders to shoot to kill any negro who refuses to surrender immediately," the *Arkansas Democrat* reported.[192]

By the time the Elaine Massacre was over, an estimated two hundred African-Americans had been killed, including men, women, and children. Five Whites had died as well, and twelve Black men were sentenced to death for their "murders." No White citizens were charged with crimes.

Michael Curry, an attorney and chair of the NAACP Advocacy and Policy Committee, summarized the proceedings best when he told *Smithsonian* magazine in 2018, "You had twelve Black men who were clearly charged with murder in a system that was absolutely corrupt at the time—you had mob influence, you had witness tampering, you had a jury that was all-White, you had almost certainly judicial bias, you had the pressure of knowing that if you were a juror in this case . . . you would almost certainly not be able to live in that town . . . if you decided anything other than a conviction."[193] The outcome was a forgone conclusion.

In February 1923, however, the unjust verdicts in Elaine led to a landmark decision by the U.S. Supreme Court. The Court ruled, by a 6-2 vote, to overturn the convictions because of "the all-White jury, lack of opportunity to testify, confessions under torture, denial of change of venue, and the pressure of the mob."[194]

After narrowly escaping the carnage in Elaine, Ike Shaw once again mustered the courage to stand up for his constitutional rights in Tyronza. He understood all too well the backlash and violence that would come with his decision, but he also knew from experience that the sharecroppers' only chance for significant change was for the Black and White men to band together.

"Aren't we all brothers and ain't God the Father of all of us?" Shaw asked the men at Sunnyside School. "We live under the same sun, eat the same food, wear the same kind of clothing, work on the same land, raise the same crop for the same landlord who oppresses and cheats us both. For a long time now the white folks and the colored folks have been fighting each other and both of us have been getting whipped all the time. We don't have nothing against one another but we got plenty against the landlord....The landlord is always betwixt us, beatin' us and starvin' us and makin' us fight each other. There ain't but one way for us to get him where he can't help himself and that's for us to get together and stay together."[195]

The STFU was organized and incorporated in Arkansas on July 26, 1934. Within six months, the union boasted having more than 4,500 members scattered throughout Arkansas, Oklahoma, and Texas. Any farmer who classified himself as a sharecropper, tenant farmer, or day laborer was eligible to join. There was no discrimination based on race, religion, or sex.

"The purpose of the union is to secure better conditions for the sharecropper, decent contracts of employment and to defend and educate the membership as to their rights under the acreage reduction contracts," STFU organizer H. L. Mitchell said at the time. "The organization hopes to secure representation on government boards set up to aid agriculture. The union is opposed to the present plantation system and hope to see this form of 'slavery' abolished."[196]

Labor unions have been around in the U.S. for at least two hundred and fifty years. The first recorded strike is believed to have occurred among New York tailors in 1768. Blacks were excluded from many early unions, such as the International Association of Machinists, which was founded in 1888—and as discussed previously, organized labor in agriculture, where Black labor was highly concentrated, didn't become popular until the 1930s.

In 1927–28, there were a few smaller strikes among melon pickers and shed packers in California, beet workers in Colorado, and greenhouse and nursery workers in Illinois.[197] But as unemployment spiked dramatically, labor unrest became more common, reaching its peak in 1933, when about 56,800 workers participated in sixty-one strikes in seventeen states.[198] Mexican onion pickers in Texas, beet workers in Michigan, citrus pickers in Florida, and cranberry pickers in Massachusetts all picketed.

After that came the Sharecroppers Union (SCU)—one of the earliest agricultural unions to include Black sharecroppers and tenants. It was organized in Tallapoosa, Alabama, in 1931 before the AAA and other New Deal federal relief programs existed. As mortgage foreclosures rose and produce prices dropped during the Great Depression, Black farmers sought help from outsiders. This stoked fears among Whites and raised suspicions in the press. *The Birmingham News* reported in July 1931 that organizers were influencing Blacks to demand "social equality with the white race, $2 a day for work, and [to] not ask but 'demand what you want, and if you don't get it, take it.'"[199]

When the U.S. Department of Labor later conducted a research study on unionism during this period, they found that the labor movement among sharecroppers and tenant farmers in the South was the work of the American Communist Party. A bulletin the federal agency published in 1945 summarizing the study's findings stated, "Self-determination of the 'Black Belt' was announced as the major objective of the Party in the South, and an ambitious program of agitation was carried out among southern Negroes."[200]

The study also found that reactions of the local community, such as those expressed in *The Birmingham News* "were duplicated many times in the South during the following years."[201]

The bulletin quoted one such source as follows, "A 'cadre' of advanced urban Negroes was trained to organize the backward colored 'peasantry,' who were to be united with the poor white population in a common class struggle of sharecroppers against landlords on the cotton plantations....Supporting these were to be urban labor unions in such industries as coal and iron mining and steel fabrication in the Birmingham area, which employed large numbers of both Negroes and whites."[202]

The U.S. Department of Labor bulletin concluded: "A union of tenants, croppers, and laborers was by its very nature a threat to the plantation system. In seeking to release these groups from dependence upon the planter and to give them a voice in renting and sharecropping contracts, the movement was 'revolutionary' and treated as such. Not only was the plantation system being menaced, but the biracial relationship of social classes was also being upset through the Negro's 'getting out of his place.' Hence the union soon faced violent suppression from growers and local authorities, aided by other resident whites."[203]

The SCU wasn't the only union in Alabama at the time. Trouble occurred at Scottsboro on July 15, 1931, when members of the Croppers' and Farm Workers Union (CFWU) met to discuss the Scottsboro Boys case, in which nine Black youths were falsely accused of raping two White women. An all-White jury sentenced the boys to death. When the Tallapoosa County sheriff learned about the meeting, he deputized a posse of Whites to break it up. Many union members were assaulted, and then the posse went to leader Ralph Gray's house and beat him and his wife.

Undeterred, the union members held a meeting the next night, and the sheriff and his posse showed up again. They were greeted by a picket line standing guard, and shots were exchanged during an argument. Someone shot the sheriff in his stomach, and Gray was wounded in both legs. Gray was taken to his house, where a posse of 150 White men found him. One of them put a gun in his mouth and fired. Four other Blacks were wounded and thirty were arrested. The posse burned Gray's house and placed his bullet-riddled body on the steps of the county courthouse as a warning to other Black laborers who might want to organize.[204]

In another incident in December 1932, the Tallapoosa County sheriff deputized a posse of more than five hundred men to track down union members who were hiding in the woods. Still, by the spring of 1933, the unions were expanding. The SCU purportedly had more than three thousand members. Two years later, it claimed to have grown to more than ten thousand with members in Georgia, Louisiana, Mississippi, and North Carolina, according to the federal bulletin.

"In the spring of that year it called a strike of cotton choppers in an attempt to raise wage rates throughout five counties. Approximately 1,500 workers were reported to have held out for almost a month for a basic wage of $1 per day. Compromise wage increases were won in several sections. According to union spokesmen a 'great wave of terror broke out against the strike,' particularly in Dallas County. Two white organizers, it was claimed, were arrested, and were beaten by a mob after being released."[205]

By this time, STFU organizers such as Mitchell and Clay East were already outspoken White socialists in Poinsett County, Arkansas. The socialists had taken up the plight of the Southern sharecroppers and tenant farmers after Norman Thomas, a six-time U.S. presidential candidate for the Socialist Party of America, toured Arkansas cotton fields earlier that year. In a column that was widely distributed in newspapers across the country, Thomas wrote that their conditions were "worse than anything in any city slum or ancient mining camp."[206]

"I found one man who after months of idleness got work on the levee," Thomas wrote. "He travelled 60 miles, leaving home at 3 a.m. and getting back at 9 p.m. His seven children are all out of school. The state runs no bus to collect them for the school in town; it provides no books, and the children have no clothes but rags. In summer they shake with malaria."[207]

When Hiram Norcross evicted additional sharecroppers and tenant farmers following the 1934 planting season, the STFU took an unprecedented step, suing him in county court on behalf of the twenty-four additional farmers who had been evicted. The plaintiffs asked a judge for a restraining order to stop evictions, as well as an order granting tenant farmers the right to cut firewood and have enough acreage to grow crops and livestock for food. The Arkansas Supreme Court eventually ruled against the tenants.

According to Conrad, a large number of Protestant ministers, both Black and White, traveled to Arkansas to assist the sharecroppers in their fight. The Southern Baptists, representing more than four million members in 24,000 churches at the time, even voted to establish a social justice bureau to investigate the "virtual peonage" in various fields, and particularly the tenant farmers and sharecroppers in the South. [208]

With the Depression in America growing deeper, the STFU expanded rapidly to include more than 25,000 members. The group was met with violence at rallies, meetings, and addresses across the South. On November 20, 1934, W.H. Stultz, president of the STFU, was arrested with three organizers in Cross County, Arkansas. They were detained for forty days until a judge ruled them not guilty.

As the STFU became more organized and attracted thousands of additional sharecroppers and tenants, the number of evictions rose, along with the incidents of violence. Stultz, the STFU president, was refused fuel by landlords and was told he would be thrown out of the one-bedroom shanty he shared with his wife and five children. On cold nights, he had to carry fuel four miles for heat. In March 1935, Stultz went into hiding after receiving death threats. He told his wife and children that four men had told him to "get out of town or we will shoot your brains out and throw your body in the St. Francis River."[209]

The union chaplain, A.B. Brookins, was arrested along with two White and one Black organizers during a meeting near Parkin, Arkansas, in December 1934. Conrad found that the county sheriff, deputies, riding bosses, and planters broke up the meeting and arrested the four. Brookins was kicked in the face and stomach and suffered permanent damage. Later, Brookins finally fled town after thirty-two shots were fired into his home.[210]

At another STFU meeting in Gilmore, Arkansas, on February 1, 1935, a college student and college director were beaten for attempting to organize about two hundred sharecroppers. "I was pulled out of the meeting and beaten with pistols and fists," the college director said. "Later, when we got back to the church, we found a 'lynch rope' the men were carrying. They apparently had lost it in the excitement."[211]

In response to the attacks and threats of lynchings, the national executive committee of the Socialist Party asked the federal government to intervene in the dispute between sharecroppers and planters. In a telegram to President Franklin D. Roosevelt, Mitchell declared that politicians would be guilty of murder if they refused to react to the "reign of terror" in Arkansas.

"Since its organization, in July, 1934, the Southern Tenant Farmers' Union, its members, officers and friends have been subjected to the most vicious and brutal attacks ever used in the stormy annals of the American labor movement," the telegraph read. "The large plantation interests of northeastern Arkansas have used every method of repression known to destroy the organization of this union....Every vestige of civil liberty is constantly denied to the class of people whom we represent. Black terror stalks the cotton field today; every vestige of democratic government has disappeared. Northeast Arkansas is as truly Fascist as Hitler's Germany."[212]

An STFU-led strike at the height of cotton-picking season in the fall of 1935 led to more than 4,000 laborers not showing up to work for ten days. The STFU held its first convention in Little Rock, Arkansas, in January 1936. By then, it had members in Oklahoma and Texas.

The preacher Howard Kester, who helped with the union's organization and recruitment of new members, wrote that meetings were banned and broken up by armed bosses; members were falsely accused, jailed, and convicted without trials; federal relief was denied; planters and their men riddled union members' homes with bullets from machine guns; Black churches and schools were burned and stuffed with hay to prevent members from meeting, and organizers were beaten and murdered. The violence spread to other states as the union's reach extended. In Hernando, Mississippi, Rev. T. A. Allen's body was found weighted down in the Coldwater River. He had been shot to death. He was wearing a coat lapel that read, "Every man a king."[213]

In March 1936, Kester published a short pamphlet entitled *Revolt among the Sharecroppers* on behalf of the STFU. Kester noted that as many as eight million Americans could have been classified as farm servants at the time.

"For nearly three-quarters of a century," Kester wrote, "sharecropping has blighted and poised the whole of southern life. . . .Of all the dreary sights in the cotton country the most pitiful are the shacks in which the tenants live. Of one, two and three rooms, they are probably the vilest places in which men have to eat and sleep in America. A few rickety chairs, a table, a bed or two, a few ragged quilts, what is left of a dresser or washstand, some broken boxes, a few broken dishes, a pig or a dog and once in a great while a few scrawny chickens usually constitute the sole possessions of a sharecropper."[214]

By banding together, Kester wrote, the STFU eliminated one of the planters' most time-worn tricks—playing the White tenants against the Blacks, and vice versa.

"Probably the presence of white men in nearly all Negro locals saved the Southern Tenant Farmers' Union from a bath of blood that would have made Hitler's campaign against the Jews resemble a Quaker prayer meeting," Kester wrote. "And there were women and children in nearly all the meetings. Even a riding boss hesitates to murder women and children—even if they are sharecroppers."[215]

CHAPTER ELEVEN

THE LAST PLANTATION

FORESIGHT IS BETTER THAN HINDSIGHT AS THE SAYING GOES. BUT A look back in time proved to be incredibly valuable in 1982, when the U.S. Commission on Civil Rights authored a scathing report about the Farmers Home Administration's (FmHA) role in the dramatic decline of Black farmers. The report's authors intended to examine the "problems confronting black farmers and the historical and current conditions—racial discrimination, lack of institutional economic support, commercial lending practices, commodity and income supports, and tax structures geared to benefit large farm operations, and others—that have contributed to the loss of black-operated farms in this country . . . ."[216]

The Commission's findings, to say the least, were stunning and all too predictable. Less than two decades earlier, in a 1965 study entitled "Equal Opportunity in Farm Programs," the Commission raised concerns that while the U.S. Department of Agriculture (USDA) had been "instrumental in raising the economic, educational, and social levels of thousands of farm and rural families . . . [a] quarter of a million Negro families stand as a glaring exception to this picture of progress."[217] Another 1979 report by the Commission found that the Farmers Home Administration decreased its housing loans to Blacks from 19.6 percent of all FmHA housing loans in 1972 to 9.5 percent only four years later.[218]

And the Commission on Civil Rights wasn't the only group putting public pressure on FmHA to improve its access to minority farmers for loans and other federal programs. In 1980, the Secretary of Agriculture's Citizens' Advisory Committee urged the USDA to "take a direct policy stance to stop the loss of minority owned farm land" and expressed particular concern about the "loss of land by Black farmers in the South." The advisory group recommended "special grant-loan-educational programs to assist low income, small farmers and help them retain their land."[219]

Yet up until the time the Commission released its 1982 report, "The Decline of Black Farming in America," very little had changed for Black farmers when it came to obtaining desperately needed financial assistance from FmHA and other federal programs.

For decades, the federal government documented incidents and complaints of discrimination against Black farmers by the USDA, particularly in its FmHA offices in predominantly White counties in the South. Black farmers reported being ridiculed, offended, and threatened. Others said they were denied opportunities to apply for loans, their applications were thrown in the trash, and that loan officers even spit on them. It's why many Black farmers still call the FmHA the "last plantation."

"The Commission finds that these FmHA credit programs have the capability to provide immediate direct assistance to black farmers to make their farms more viable and to prevent further loss of their lands," the report said. "However, FmHA has not given adequate emphasis or priority to the crisis facing black farmers; thus, despite their disproportionate need, black farmers are not fully benefiting from FmHA loan programs. In some cases, FmHA may have hindered the efforts of black small farm operators to remain a viable force in agriculture. Furthermore, as the Commission has found in the past, USDA and FmHA have failed to integrate civil rights goals into program objectives and to use enforcement mechanisms to ensure that black farmers are provided equal opportunities in farm credit programs."[220]

At the time the report was published, there were only 57,271 farms being operated by Blacks in the U.S.; that was only 6.2 percent of the nearly 926,000 Black-operated farms that existed at its peak in 1920. Nearly 94 percent of Black-operated farms had been lost since 1920; White-run farms had decreased by 56.4 percent during that time.[221] Black farmers had also lost nearly twice as much land as their White counterparts. The researchers found that the "escalation of land values is such that black-owned land is increasingly targeted by land speculators and developers. 'The frequent pattern is for land to remain in minority hands only so long as it is economically marginal, and then to be acquired by whites when its value begins to increase.'"[222]

"Historically, racial discrimination in credit and in the selling of land has resulted in smaller and less productive landholdings for blacks," the Commission reported. "These disadvantages have been compounded by current lending practices, research, technology, commodity price and income supports, and tax structures which are geared to benefit large farm operations. Thus, black farm operators have been placed in increasingly disadvantageous and noncompetitive positions vis-a-vis predominantly white large farm operators."[223]

The Commission reported that the FmHA had approved nearly $7 billion in farm loan programs in fiscal year 1981. Of that amount, Blacks received only 5.1 percent of the total number of loans and only 2.5 percent of the total dollar amount loaned. The average loan for White farmers was $39,082 ... which was more than twice as much as the average loan for Blacks farmers at $18,290.[224]

Specifically, the Commission found that Black farmers were at competitive disadvantage because their farms were so much smaller than those owned by Whites. In 1978, the average commercial

Black-operated farm was 128 acres; the average White-operated farm was more than three times as big at 428 acres.[225] "The relatively small size of their landholdings combine with current economic conditions, governmental policies, and institutional practices to place black farmers at a competitive disadvantage with large farm operators and investors, most of whom are white," the commission found. "Economies of scale, research and technology, tax benefits, government price and income supports, and commercial lending all militate against the survival of black-operated small farms."[226]

The Commission found that federal agricultural research conducted by land-grant colleges and universities, which was being financed by public tax dollars, was geared toward larger, more efficient, White-owned commercial farms. It also concluded that discriminatory federal funding had precluded historically Black colleges and universities from conducting research to aid Black farmers. In fact, although HBCUs have been in existence since 1890, they didn't receive federal money for agricultural research until 1972. White land-grant universities, first founded in 1862, started receiving such funds in 1887.[227] Even when the federal government allocated discretionary money to HBCUs for agricultural research between 1967 and 1971, it was one-half of 1 percent of the funding that Congress had authorized to White land-grant colleges, according to the Commission's report.[228]

Black farmers were also adversely impacted by the commodity and price and income support programs that were created during the New Deal and were still alive in the seventies. The Commission found that price and direct income support payments mostly went to large White farm operators—the farmers who needed them least. The smallest 30 percent of farmers who received them were allocated only 4 percent of all payments. The payments ranged from $365 for small farmers to $36,000 for the largest with more than 2,500 acres.[229]

"Thus, large farmers benefit most from farm commodity programs, which in turn enhances their ability to borrow and invest capital in more land and improved technology, resulting in increased production on their part and a progressively increasing disadvantage for small farmers," the report said. "The U.S. Department of Agriculture, in its report on the structure of agriculture, acknowledged that these government programs may contribute to the loss of small farms."[230]

Conversely, Black farmers had faced discriminatory lending practices, from both private local banks and federal loan programs, for several decades. According to the 1974 U.S. Census, the average farm debt for all Southern commercial farmers was $44,600, but only $12,888 for Black farmers.[231] It wasn't that Black farmers weren't trying to borrow as much money to acquire more land, better equipment, and more enhanced seeds and fertilizers; it's that banks and federal officials wouldn't loan them the money. Insurance companies, which made the majority of farm loans in the U.S. at the time, required loans to be at least $100,000. Commercial banks required loans to be repaid within five years, and federal land banks required amounts of collateral that Black farmers didn't have.

The 1982 report from the U.S. Commission on Civil Rights concluded its assessment of FmHA with these blistering words: "And finally, financial institutions, including the Farmers Home Administration, have a reputation of discriminatory lending, which poses a real, as well as a psychological, barrier for blacks."[232]

The Commission cited a 1981 survey of 147 Black landowners in Tennessee, which found that 96 percent of respondents believed that Black land loss was the result of illegal means.[233] Furthermore, 88 percent of the Black landowners attributed the land loss to the "refusal of mortgage companies to make loans to Blacks" and "persons in official capacities working together to gain possession of Black-owned lands."[234]

"This deep distrust, combined with lack of knowledge regarding possible loan programs, prevents blacks from utilizing much needed lending sources," the Commission found. "For example, in another survey of black landowners in the South, fewer than 15 percent of the respondents had ever applied for agricultural loans through the Farmers Home Administration—the institution with loan programs created to meet most appropriately the needs of these struggling farmers."[235]

Another deep-rooted problem among Black farmers, according to the Commission, was that many of them were farming on heir property—land they had inherited without a will. In the past, when Black landowners died, they rarely left wills because of their deep-rooted distrust in the legal system and inability to pay attorneys' fees. As a result, many farms didn't have clear titles or ownership. "Land passed down through generations without the existence of wills frequently is conveyed among an extended family of cousins, aunts, and uncles in a complex division of ownership," the commission report said. "No one individual holds title to the heir property. Often, heirs move out of the area; sometimes their whereabouts are unknown."[236]

A 1978 study commissioned by the U.S. Department of Agriculture and conducted by the Emergency Land Fund (ELF) found that 27 percent of all Black-owned property in the Southeast was heir property. An average of eight people jointly owned the properties, and an average of five of those people had moved outside the Southeast.[237]

A lack of clear ownership leaves heir property highly susceptible to partition and tax sales, according to the Commission. In some cases, a single heir can ask a judge to auction off the entire parcel of land if the heirs can't reach an agreement on how to divide the land and sell it. The land can then be purchased by an outside bidder at auction if a single heir can't afford to purchase the entire parcel.

"In some cases, the land is bought below market price by a speculator who initially urged one of the heirs to sell his/her interest," the report said. "Thus, heir property may fall prey to 'sharp' practices, 'practices which are, although technically legal, clearly unscrupulous.'" The ELF noted that the "purchasers at these [partition and] tax sales are almost always white persons, frequently local lawyers or relatives of local officials, who make it their business to keep abreast of what properties are going to auction and who attend the auctions prepared to buy."[238]

The Farmers Home Administration was originally created as the Resettlement Administration as part of President Franklin Roosevelt's New Deal in 1935. Its purpose was to assist the rural poor to "re-establish themselves on a self-supporting basis." During a two-year period, the Resettlement Administration provided more than 300,000 loans. The Resettlement Administration became the Farm Security Administration (FSA) as part of the 1937 Bankhead-Jones Farm Tenant Act, which authorized forty-year loans for farmers "unable to obtain credit elsewhere to buy land or improve their farms and homes." The FSA made more than 13,000 loans between 1937 and 1941.[239] Five years later, the FSA became FmHA as part of the Farmers Home Administration Act.

In 1981, FmHA had a national office under the U.S. Department of Agriculture, forty-six state offices, more than three hundred district offices, and approximately 1,800 county offices in the fifty states and other U.S. territories.[240] The administrator for FmHA appointed state directors, who oversaw district directors and allocated federal money to the states. The district directors supervised the county officials, who were the primary point of contact for farmers seeking FmHA loans.

The Commission found that FmHA granted almost $13 billion in loans in 1980, including $6.3 billion in farm loans.[241] Even though Congress intended for FmHA to be the "lender of last resort" and a source for borrowers who couldn't get help elsewhere, the Commission concluded that FmHA officials were routinely ignoring safeguards that were in place to ensure that FmHA loans were only being awarded to borrowers who couldn't get assistance elsewhere.

"[T]o ensure that FmHA serves only those who are unable to obtain loans from other sources, 'credit elsewhere' tests are applied to loan applicants," the Commission wrote in its report. "However, the lack of alternative credit may be self-certified by the applicant or based on the judgment of the county supervisor. The decision to require documentation is discretionary and prone to influence by subjective factors, such as personal relationships and status in the community."[242]

In other words, the good-old-boy system was alive and well in the South. A General Accounting Office (GAO) study found that in a "significant number of instances, 'credit elsewhere' tests were never applied and many FmHA borrowers could have found sources of credit other than FmHA."[243]

"Upon reviewing 200 rejected and approved housing loan files in 15 county offices, GAO found 'various disparities in the criteria adopted.' Variations were found in job tenure requirements and verification of credit-worthiness. It is likely that determinations of eligibility for farm loans are equally subjective, for example, with respect to required farm experience, credit-worthiness, property appraisals, and viability of farm plans. Lack of specific criteria for loan determination potentially enhances FmHA's flexibility and ability to serve clients. It also creates loopholes which allow for discriminatory treatment."[244]

The Commission discovered that there had been eighty-five equal opportunity complaints filed in 1980 concerning farm operating and farm ownership loans. In one complaint filed by farmers in North Carolina, Black farmers complained that they had been the victims of discrimination and were subjected to "disrespect, embarrassment, and humiliation" by FmHA officials. The farmers alleged that they were denied opportunities to submit loan applications; were approved for less money that what they had applied for; sometimes received less money than their loans were approved for; had loan repayment schedules accelerated for no reason; and that county FmHA officials were contacting banks and other creditors and informing them that loans wouldn't be approved for the Black farmers, thus denying them credit, services, and goods needed to operate their farms.[245]

A U.S. Department of Agriculture inquiry concluded that Black farmers in Gates and Hertford counties in North Carolina typically received less money than White farmers and that minorities waited "inordinate periods" for loan approvals.[246] The USDA found that of the forty-one outstanding FmHA loans in Gates County on September 30, 1979, Blacks had received only six, compared to thirty-five for Whites. The average Black loan was $23,300; the average White loan was $116,860. According to the report, Blacks had only received "emergency" loans, while Whites were awarded ownership, operating, and emergency aid. Even more alarming was that six Black farmers, despite having an average of ten years in farming, were unaware of the emergency loan program. One Black farmer suffering from economic hardship was told no emergency loan program existed and was advised to seek employment at a chicken processing plant. Conversely, a 21-year-old White farmer secured $247,000 in such loans. Two Black farmers were required to agree to voluntary liquidation as a loan condition.[247]

The USDA also uncovered what was commonplace in FmHA county offices: even though Gates County's population of 8,524 was

54 percent Black, there were no Blacks on the FmHA committee that oversaw the loan programs. George Norman Jr., a Black farmer there, told *The News & Observer* in Raleigh, North Carolina, that there were only thirty-four Black farmers left in 1982, down from 169 in 1954. Part of the problem, according to Norman, was that Black landowners were renting their land to Whites because they could get financing and pay taxes, while Blacks could not. His father, George Norman Sr., had to sell the breeding stock of his hog operation to repay FmHA loans.

"That killed his spirit," Norman Jr. said, "because he had raised hogs since he was a boy."[248]

An earlier federal statewide class-action lawsuit filed by two Black farmers in Mississippi accused the FmHA and its state director of discrimination in granting loans to Black farmers, of similar discrimination against small farmers, and of failing to follow statutory and regulatory requirements, specifically those mandating special help and supervisory assistance to "limited resources applicants." Rubin Hudson, one of the plaintiffs, said he was on the verge of losing his 300-acre farm to foreclosure because FmHA had refused to make him loans of the size needed to operate his farm. He alleged that FmHA had made his financial situation worse by advertising his farm to other farmers and banks in the area as potentially being for sale, and that the agency had advised him to sell his land and farm equipment. Edward Fant, the other complainant, alleged that FmHA waited too long to approve his loan, causing him to miss the maximum yield from his land. He had been denied a loan in October 1978 because the funds weren't available, and when he reapplied three months later, the FmHA waited five months to approve it.

According to the *Clarion-Ledger* in Jackson, Mississippi, the "suit charges the FmHA makes loans based on political associations of the applicants and to farmers who are ineligible under provisions requiring the loans go only to farmers unable to get loans from banks and other sources."[249]

At the time, the U.S. Commission on Civil Rights found that Blacks comprised only 7.3 percent of the FmHA's total employees and that the number of Black loan specialists had declined from 6.8 percent to 4.8

percent between 1977 and 1980.[250] There was also limited representation for Blacks on the FmHA county committees, which determined the eligibility of applicants and how much money they could borrow.

According to the report, only 4.3 percent of all FmHA county committee members were Black in 1980. From 1979 to 1980, the number of Black county committee members fell from 427 to 257, while the total number of members increased from 5,863 to 5,966.[251] The loss of Black representatives was even more profound at the state level, where "Tennessee lost 93.3 percent of its black committee members, Georgia, 60.7 percent; Mississippi, 56.3 percent; and Alabama, 48.6 percent."[252]

The Commission's report was published about a year after a high-profile incident in Covington, Tennessee, in which a group of Black farmers staged a sit-in at the FmHA office in Tipton County. A group of twelve farmers occupied the office for more than three weeks and refused to leave. The group's leader, Thomas Burrell, were protesting lag times for their applications for farm operating loans. FmHA investigators met with the farmers but couldn't persuade them to leave. "You can't plant a crop with an investigation," Burrell told reporters at the time.[253]

Burrell's nephew, Shelby Burrell, joined him in the protest. Shelby Burrell had been farming 383 acres for two years, growing cotton and soybeans. He graduated from the University of Tennessee-Martin with a music degree. He said the FmHA denied him a loan because of his lack of farming experience, even though he grew up on the family farm. He moved to Michigan for a year before returning to farm with his uncle. He applied for another FmHA loan for $97,000 in October 1979.

"[T]hen it hit delay after delay after delay," Shelby said. "The loan was approved that December, but they told me later they didn't have any more money. They'd already loaned it out."[254] Finally, the FmHA approved a $64,000 loan in August 1980, but it was too late for him to plant.

The Black farmers ended their sit-in in early April 1981. Their protest concluded with a rally at the FmHA office. Similar gatherings were held at FmHA offices in other Southern states and as far away as Iowa, Nebraska, New York, and Washington. The group traveled to

Washington, D.C., the next week to meet with the U.S. Secretary of Agriculture and other politicians.

Joseph Brooks, then head of the Emergency Land Fund, told reporters at the time that Black farmers were losing their land because they couldn't get financing. The protest came at a time when President Ronald Reagan was threatening to cut the FmHA's funding.

"Black farmers are being forced off their lands because they can't get financing," Brooks said. "The situation in Covington highlights what's behind it. The agency has gotten away from its mandate as a financial institution of last resort for small farmers....Black farmers were already at the end of the line. If this goes through, they'll be completely out of the line."[255]

PART THREE

A SENSE OF JUSTICE

CHAPTER TWELVE

———•———

DETERMINED PURPOSE

I T TOOK TIME, BUT JUST AS THE STRUGGLE THAT BEGAN IN THE FIELDS was taken up in the union halls, and later in the executive and legislative branches of government, it would finally be taken up in the courts too. There were several people whose pursuit of justice influenced *Pigford v. Glickman* and Pigford II in some way. As it happened, each was a member of the youngest generation in their families at the time. Whether they were farmers themselves, or they were fighting on behalf of loved ones who were, each strongly identified with their family's farming history. And each was taking responsibility to help move Black farming forward for future generations. This is the long arc of identity at its best. Gary Grant is one such justice seeker. His story began with an incident in his childhood ...

Gary watched with fascination as the tractors rumbled toward his home. The drivers were ready to shut down their vehicles after a long day on the 1,500 acres of farmland that his parents operated in northeast

North Carolina. The boy watched them kick up dust and marveled at the new equipment. The tractors reached the start of the driveway and made the move that demonstrated the man was in control over the machine. Each of the drivers took hold of the lever right under the steering wheel to accelerate and turn into the driveway of his home. Then they gunned it out to the shelter.

Driving one of those machines would prove that he was more than a farm boy, Gary thought. His parents had taught him how to feed the chickens and slop the hogs. He gathered eggs. He chopped the fields, picked cotton, and shook peanuts with his mother while his dad plowed behind the mule. Then in the early 1950s, the first tractor arrived. He dreamed of climbing up into the driver's seat and clutching the lever. He waited for the day when he could bring a tractor home. His brothers did too. Then one afternoon, his father finally let Gary bring one in. There he was, a young boy sitting on the throne of the four wheels. Fulfilling his destiny. Being a farmer. He propelled the tractor easily all the way back to his house and reached the point where he could see the driveway. Then he mimicked the move that he had watched so many times before. Place hand on the lever. Push the lever up. Then gun it. Before he knew it, he had reached the barn where the tractors were sheltered. But it wasn't time to celebrate the victory of his first tractor drive yet. The vehicle wouldn't stop. He panicked as it proved *it* was in control. It barreled toward the pasture fence. Gary was useless at this point. He was no longer able to commandeer the tractor. All he could do was hang on as it plowed straight through a fence. The vehicle kept going until it hit a ditch that ran through the middle of the pasture.

The wild ride was over. But about a third of the fence was gone. What would his father say, he wondered? Gary's dad, Matthew Grant, didn't typically curse. He didn't typically raise his voice either. He was a calm, unassuming man. Gary knew his dad loved and supported his children. But Gary didn't know what something like this would do to a man. The cost to repair a fence? The embarrassment of having his son unable to drive a tractor? Gary listened for the one phrase—"John Brown"—that often indicated to him and his siblings that they were in big trouble. Would his dad mutter that name? When his father approached, he didn't yell, curse or even say "John Brown." He checked to see if Gary was hurt. Gary, fortunately, wasn't harmed, but that still didn't make it a good time for a lesson. His dad called someone else over to drive the tractor back to its place. He put his arm around Gary, making the boy feel the kind of warmth that only comes from the familiarity of family. He then put his hand on Gary's shoulder and said, "Son, you know if you don't get some education, you are going to starve to death."[256]

Gary took him at his word. He never volunteered to drive a tractor again, and his dad never asked him either. His brothers drove the tractors and spent hours in the sun breaking land and planting. The only wheel he got behind was the wheel of a truck he used to pick up the help hired to pick cotton and dig peanuts from the soil. The tractor incident became part of the lore he told decades later, after seeing his parents forced to give up farming.

Both Gary's dad and his mother, Florenza Moore Grant, were avid outdoors people and gardeners. When they got married after high school, they moved to Newport News, Virginia, where Gary's dad got a job with a dry dock ship builder. But the lure of farm life in their home state of North Carolina, and all they were hearing about a federal government program there, were too strong. President Franklin Delano Roosevelt's New Deal initiatives in 1936 created resettlement communities that offered people forty acres and a mule. Tillery, North Carolina, a hub for sharecroppers and Black families to farm on former plantation properties following the Civil War, became one of the estimated 113 resettlement communities. Tillery was in Halifax County, just one county away from where Matthew and Florenza grew up, right across the Roanoke River, and less than thirty miles from the Virginia state line. Those who participated in the resettlement community were loaned land, livestock, a house, and tools for at least three years. During that time, they learned to farm, participate in the community, and show their level of interest, commitment, and potential to the government. Once they did that, they'd earn the title and pay the rest of the loan over a forty-year period.

Gary's mother was a descendant of landowning Whites and sharecropping Blacks. Her great-grandfather was German and her great-grandmother was Native American. His dad's family were land-owners after slavery ended. When the Grants heard about the reset-tlement community near their childhood homes, they traveled down from Newport News to Tillery. There were still 18,000 acres available, so the Grants were able to acquire 60 acres of land *and* a house with such comforts as electricity. They were hopeful as they joined other Black families in this still relatively new community. This land held the promise of providing financial independence and a legacy. But there already were tensions when they arrived. The resettlement community was segregated. The Whites had been moved out of the flood plains. The Grants' land, much like the land of the other Black people, was on the flood side of the Roanoke River, which posed a threat to their livelihood. Wiregrass covered so much of the property that it had to be hauled out by the wagonload and burned before the farmland was usable.

Eventually, close to 300 families settled in that community. The government had included everything Gary's parents thought they needed: a community center with a stage that seated 600 people, a health clinic with equipment for X-rays, a potato curing house, a grist mill, and a community store. Gary, who was born on August 19, 1943, was just a few years old when his parents moved to Tillery. He had an older brother and sister, and then two siblings followed. He and his siblings played marbles and dodgeball. They rolled tires. They walked on stilts made of tin cans that they controlled with hay baling wires. His childhood seemed happy, enjoyable, even normal. But then came natural disasters, such as Hurricane Hazel in 1959. And, of course, there was the arrival of industrialization and the mechanization of farming. You had to own the new equipment just to stay competitive, but you also needed larger tracts of land to optimize their use and expense. Some farmers didn't make it under such pressures. Gary's parents, however, were entrepreneurs, progressives, and visionaries. They knew they had to expand their land. They were also partners: His dad was the farmer, but his mother won over the bankers with her looks. She was attrac-tive and used her seamstress skills to make sure that she *and* her chil-dren were fashionable. She made most of the family's clothes, including his sister's prom dress and wedding gown. One time, another family in the community wore the Sunday suits she made for Gary and his brothers to attend their father's funeral. She showed her children that she was strong and outspoken. Florenza was the first Black woman in the community to have a driver's license. She was also the first Black woman in the resettlement community to register to vote.

The Grants ended up with 400 acres of peanuts, which was their "cash crop" since the White side of the resettlement community had the tobacco farms. (According to Gary, peanuts became "the good cash crop" on Black farms after the government gave the tobacco allotments to the White people with the high ground.) The Grants also had 200 acres of cotton, 300 acres of soybeans, and 400 acres of corn. They were considered "top middle class" among the Black farmers. They had control over their own lives, but they still earned lower prices than Whites when they sold their produce or commodities. Peanuts sold for 10.9 cents a pound, but the White men would say, "Oh, that .9 doesn't mean anything."[257]

The governmental loan programs also seemed to favor Whites. His family's loans for the tractors and equipment came with a stipulation: anything they gained during the life of that loan became collateral for the loan. If they borrowed on their forty acres and accumulated another forty acres, and then a disaster happened, they couldn't mortgage the second forty because it served as collateral. That's one reason why his parents didn't rely on farming as their sole source of income. His dad became a licensed barber and opened a barber shop. They ran a service station in the White part of a nearby community named Scotland Neck. They also owned a casket company. At times, these were the alternatives to Gary's father joining other men on their early morning travels to Hogs Island, Virginia, to help build a nuclear power plant in the late 1960s and early 1970s.

Their children, including Gary, went to college. Following the advice his dad offered years earlier when he hit the fence with the tractor, Gary focused his studies on something other than agriculture. He worked on the farm to pay for college, turning the cotton into cash for tuition. Although his parents wanted their children to be doctors and lawyers, he studied dramatic arts and English at then-North Carolina

College, now North Carolina Central University. As a college student, he was excited to be arrested for civil disobedience for the first time. He was trained in nonviolent protests and marched with about 500 other students in Durham with the Rev. Martin Luther King Jr. The Howard Johnson hotel and restaurant on the interstate was where he was taken into custody. He would be arrested nineteen more times after that. And about forty years later, in 2020, after civil rights legends including MLK, the Rev. Joseph Lowery, and U.S. Rep. John Lewis had passed, he would admit that King's dream had not been a reality, saying, "We've got another 100 years at least before that happens, looking at where things are now. When communities and towns finally come together to sit down and talk about racism, then real progress can be made. It's hurtful that this hasn't happened to this day."[258]

After earning his bachelor of arts degree, he yearned for a bigger stage. That stage was Broadway. Although he spent time in New York City, he saw the struggles most Black men who wanted to be actors endured. In 1965, when his summer with a Shakespeare troupe in Ohio ended, he returned home to Tillery where a teaching job was open at the local elementary school. When he applied for that job, he mentioned his dad's reputation in the community, particularly as a Black farmer. He had known for years that farming was a risky and expensive endeavor and was proud of his family for having powered through all the challenges.

Although foreclosures were common, he never expected what happened in 1971 would set off a five-decade long battle between his family and the federal government.

That year, his parents borrowed from the USDA's Farmers Home Administration. It was a five-year loan, but during that time period, three of those years were declared disaster years in their community. Their loans were already at higher interest rates than loans granted to White farmers. The late payments accumulated. In September 1976, the agriculture department foreclosed on his parents. They owed $47,000.

The Grants had only ever heard of Black farmers being foreclosed on. Only one White family that they knew of fell under the same scrutiny, and they rented land and had equipment, but did not own the land. The Grants believed this second-class treatment was something they should not accept. Gary and his siblings joined his parents to find a solution. That farm helped pay their college tuitions. The family had taken no welfare from the government. His dad often said, "The only legacy the Black farmer had to leave his children was the land."[259] Four of the Grant children had graduated college by then and were working public jobs. They offered to assume the loan but were refused. They also offered the Farmers Home Administration a cash settlement in the foreclosure negotiations, but there were no negotiations.

In 1981, the state FmHA director, district director, and local FmHA agent told his dad that it didn't matter who he went to see or who he brought to their office on his behalf. If he didn't come up with all of the money, he was going to be sold out. He was an honest, good, Christian man who wanted to pay his debt. The worst was watching his father be told there was nothing he could do. Gary's family was "a true middle class success story until the United States Department of Agriculture decided, 'We want that riverfront property back.'"[260]

Gary became a man with a new purpose.

He advocated for Black farmers before, but this was a personal crusade that would ultimately take him from his family's land to the White House.

As if Gary and his family weren't facing enough challenges, a year later he learned that the county planned to close the school where he taught. He soon began working full-time for his parents at Tillery Casket Manufacturers Incorporated, which employed twelve people, though that was about half of the help they could have used. At the time, he was also weighing whether or not to help form the Concerned Citizens of Tillery, in response to the decision to shut down the school. He could see the organization becoming a group with power and respect. He could also have a starring role.

He was good at mobilizing for change. Over the years, he helped register Black voters. He also helped Black candidates run for office. And to fight the pending foreclosure of his parents' land, he helped his family make civil rights complaints against the USDA and the former Farmers Home Administration.

In 1983, he created the Land Loss Fund to provide education, research, and other assistance that would help Black farmers, who were receiving miniscule amounts of loans and research funds, keep their land. The grassroots effort joined farmers with social workers, business-people, educators, and others. He believed the USDA agents' discrim-inatory practices needed to be exposed. To accomplish this goal, he needed the battle to be more than one family's fight. However, that wouldn't happen for another fifteen years.

Debt mounted. Interest and penalties on his parents' loan started to double and triple the amount they owed. Attorneys' fees eventu-ally added to the debt too. Over a thirty-year period, what was owed grew to $171,000. He saw all the silent signs of intimidation in official places. Nooses hung on the wall in some USDA agent's offices. In 1995, his father went for his last appeal hearing before the USDA. When the man representing the USDA came in, he was wearing a tie with patterned images of Confederate soldiers waving the Confederate flag on it. What gall he had to come into a room saying he was representing the U.S. government in that manner and telling a Black man he would deal justly with him, Gary thought. The message to Blacks was that "They should stay in their place."[261] In 1996, the USDA didn't execute a final judgment—even though it was signed by the USDA's Office of Civil Rights—that focused on four years of discrimination against Gary's parents.

In April 1997, Gary took his story to Washington, D.C., upon the invitation of the Congressional Black Caucus. There he shared his expe-rience of federal loan discrimination. He sat at a wide table in a room with nearly every seat behind him occupied by Black men and teens. He faced members of Congress and Agriculture Secretary Dan Glickman. Over a button-down shirt, Gary wore a white T-shirt that featured what appeared to be a black-and-white photo of his mother. His comments were written down, but he didn't seem to need the notes. "There are two issues that need to be very clear here today. One is discrimination and the other is racism. Discrimination against small family farmers across this nation and the racism that's perpetuated by white, uh racist, bigots who administer the offices, especially in the rural south," he said.[262]

He paused his monologue, fully expecting the applause that followed. He didn't even look behind him, but knowing teenage boys were in the room, he asked Congresswoman Maxine Waters, the caucus chair from California, for permission to ask them to stand up. About ten did so. Their lives, he said, are being ruined because of discrimination and racism. When the USDA began the "social experiment" of resettlement communities, it gave Black families an opportunity to get the land, but now it's doing everything it possibly can to take it away from us, he told the panel.

It had taken a toll on his family for twenty-six years. His mother and father were ailing with no source of income. Of the 300 Black farm families that settled in Tillery when his parents did, none was still farming. On TV, the words underneath his name called Gary "A Black Farmer." Though he wasn't actively farming the land, he could have been. It wasn't the tractor incident that kept him from being a second-generation farmer or that robbed his nephew of a future in farming. He blamed the USDA for that fact. The men in that agency took away their livelihood. His parents—once entrepreneurs and visionaries—didn't have energy or many years left to fight.

His family had been able to stave off the USDA for more than two decades. His father was now 78. Gary paused. His brows knitted together, and his eyes were cast down behind his wire-rimmed glasses. His mother was 75, he said. He placed his hands on his mouth and then on his chin. He pursed his lips, either to keep sobs or anger from erupting. They dared to stand for what was right. They had suffered enough humiliation. More than anything, Gary wanted to have his parents' case resolved before they died. Losing the farms would eventually mean losing a way of life and losing communities that had provided a sense of happiness for decades before. "Enough is enough," he said.[263] He received a standing ovation from the crowd and fellow farmers, including John Boyd Jr., the founder and president of the nonprofit National Black Farmers Association. John was all too familiar with the challenges Gary spoke about. He had been forced into bankruptcy after he had been unable to secure a loan from the USDA for his farm. He filed a civil rights complaint about his local field office with the USDA and discovered other discrimination cases, some dating well before the Grant family, in his attempt to settle that complaint.

That hearing wouldn't be the last time they were together in Washington, D.C.

CHAPTER THIRTEEN

———

JOURNEY TO JUSTICE

J OHN BOYD JR. HAD SUFFERED TREMENDOUS FINANCIAL DISTRESS
and knew many other Black farmers who had been mistreated and
ignored by the U.S. Department of Agriculture before he was invited
to speak to members of Congress in 1997. His thoughts on the subject
were very clear: enough debt. Enough suffering. Enough discrimination.

He had been spat on. He had seen his loan application ripped up
and thrown in the trash. He had listened to the USDA's county representatives—the men with the power to essentially decide between a
future and foreclosure—berate Black men and flatter fellow White men
in the same office. He had been called racial slurs. Years later, he became
a sought-after voice for Black farmers, appearing on CNN and quoted
regularly by traditional and Black media outlets. He posed for photos
with Presidents Bill Clinton and Barack Obama, made a bid for the
U.S. House of Representatives, spoke out on voter suppression and U.S.

trade agreements, and boycotted companies such as John Deere and Wachovia because he saw that they lacked inclusiveness.

But in 1997—as he introduced other Black farmers and the family members representing them (including Gary Grant) to legislators—he pleaded for fair and equitable, across-the-board settlements for all Black farmers who had proven discrimination in the USDA loans process. "The settlement process is totally, totally unacceptable by putting the poor Black farmer on the fence as though this person has committed another crime," he told U.S. Secretary of Agriculture Dan Glickman and congressional leaders at that hearing.[264] He had received dozens of phone calls—averaging sixty a day at that point—from Black farmers wondering when the USDA would respond to their discrimination complaints that had been on file for as many as five years. He believed the way the complaints were handled was yet another terrible, horrible offense against Black farmers, continuing the pain and suffering they had endured for more than 130 years. The number of Black farmers continued to decline, down to about 18,000, representing less than 1 percent of farmers in the U.S. The harsh reality is that Boyd may be the last generation in his family to farm.

Farmers did not need to be put on the defensive any longer, he urged.

Boyd, who eventually owned nearly 400 acres in rural Virginia and raised beef cattle and farmed corn, tobacco, soybeans, and wheat, had always imagined that the rest of his life would be spent on a farm, far away from lawsuits and legislators.[265] Growing up he didn't want to be an attorney or a doctor. He wanted to be a farmer, just like his parents, grandparents, and great-grandfather before him. During the summers, he would travel from his home in Queens, New York, where he was born in 1965, to visit his grandparents' land in Mecklenburg County, Virginia. There he watched his grandfathers on their farm. His maternal grandfather was a sharecropper and his great-grandfather was a slave. When he was a teenager, his parents moved to Virginia, providing him ample opportunity to learn even more about farming from his father and his grandparents. His father acknowledged that there was "something about farming that got in his blood and he never let go."[266] He wanted to treat the land well. His forebears repeated this mantra: "The land knows no color. It does not discriminate against anyone. The land doesn't mistreat anyone. Land is power."[267] The land that his grandfather and great-grandfather worked showed they had a "rightful place in this country."[268] They earned it. Farming was for everybody, he believed, in his youthful naivety.

Boyd was so excited about owning farmland—after all, his father taught him that land is the "most important tool that a person can possess."[269] That excitement, combined with his competitive edge, led him to get started as a farmer before he even turned 20. He purchased 210 acres in Baskerville, Virginia, in the same county where he spent his summers and then his teenage years. By 1985, when he was just 19 years old, he became a fourth-generation farmer. The cost? He incurred a $50,000 debt from the Farmers Home Administration, a USDA program.[270] The farm was rundown, but Boyd was confident he knew how to improve it. He started with soybeans and livestock.

Like many farmers, he needed an operating loan for the funds to plant his crops on time. He needed money for fertilizer, for seed, for equipment. All this was necessary for a maximum harvest and the best yields. It was the late 1980s and this was his first foray into trying to work with the USDA.

Wednesday was the day when the loan supervisor in his county would see farmers. On those days, Black farmers gathered in the lobby. It was called "Black Wednesday." They knew one another but didn't discuss the others' loan situations. They would hear the denials though. The supervisor would leave the door open wide enough so people could hear him talk down to the Black farmer meeting with him. When a White farmer came in, the Black farmers would be kicked out of the office. The door would be closed. Private. Quiet. That's how their conservation went. Then the door would stay open and the volume would increase again when the next Black farmer entered the office. Public. Loud. Boyd would be told, "Boy, I need you to go on out of here."[271] Boyd didn't understand why he couldn't get a loan. He couldn't understand why one year, the supervisor tore up his application in front of him and threw it in the garbage. He told Boyd he wasn't going to process the loan.

"Well, why not? I think I'm qualified for the loan."

"Well, I don't have any money to lend you—any of my money," he told Boyd.[272]

The supervisor often used that phrase "my money." But it wasn't his. It was the federal government's money. Farmers expected to endure acts of nature—the droughts, the tornadoes, the hurricanes. "But you never should be faced with the actual hand of the federal government," Boyd thought.[273] The government was supposed to give you a lending hand up, not mistreat you.

Denied. Denied again. And again. For nine years. He was told there were no funds for him. But he saw White farmers getting loans from the USDA. In one year, 147 loans were given in his county; only two of them were to Black farmers. He wasn't sure if the loan officer didn't like him or if racism was the root of the denials. He had always wanted to farm, but he had to turn to other ways to make money. He was a prison guard, a welder, and a janitor. His family gave him money. So did a tobacco warehouse owner. But he wouldn't accept the "no" from the USDA without seeking why. He filed discrimination complaints with the civil rights office in his county.

In 1994, his efforts seemed to hit a dead end when the government foreclosed on his farm and stuck a "For Sale" sign in his yard. In frustration, Boyd sawed the sign in half. He had lost his poultry contract. He had divorced. His ex-wife and son moved to Richmond, Virginia. He declared bankruptcy. And he was only 28 years old. He felt "helpless."[274]

He pursued what was probably his one last resort: a lawsuit. Then as he waited for a response to the federal suit filed through his local civil rights office, he started to realize it wasn't just him. Other Black farmers believed they faced losses because of loan discrimination too. The USDA treated them unfairly "by taking land from Black farmers—one, by not lending them enough money to tend and harvest their crops, and two, by not lending them any money at all."[275]

No organization seemed to be willing to help, so he decided to create the National Black Farmers Association in 1995. The association's motto was, "We have our mule, now we're looking for our 40 acres."

Two years later, in May 1997, Boyd's personal lawsuit was settled. The USDA found that he had indeed been discriminated against in the loan process. He was awarded $1 million in debt relief and cash. His persistence paid off. "Man, now I can go home and just finish farming," he thought. He knew farming was tough, whether you're Black or White. But racism and discrimination made it nearly impossible for him to retreat. He knew many Black farmers who had died waiting for justice. As he discovered in his own legal battle, the backlog of discrimination cases dated to the 1960s. The agriculture department appeared to overlook or destroy discrimination complaints after its civil rights office experienced cutbacks in 1983. When the Clinton administration reopened the Office of Civil Rights and Glickman formed a new USDA civil rights team in 1996, Boyd was told that some boxes of complaints had never been processed. Two inches of dust covered them. The USDA had "acknowledged discrimination before in letters to individual farmers," *The Richmond Times-Dispatch* noted, but a "general public acknowledgment is rare."[276]

Boyd had already organized in late 1996 a group of about sixty farmers who journeyed to Washington, D.C., to protest racial discrimination in the USDA, landing a meeting with Glickman. These farmers had been overlooked for decades and could not be overlooked any longer, he thought. Just as he had envisioned creating a farm operation that would be bigger, better and more efficient, he committed to using his aggressive and competitive nature to find a way to help and advocate for Black farmers. They contributed to the fabric of American agriculture. They should not be denied the ability to participate in federal programs. That decision took him back and forth from his Virginia farm to Washington, D.C., for decades.

In early 1997, Glickman and the USDA's civil rights action team held a series of twelve listening sessions nationwide; Boyd attended them along with James Myart, who at that point, was serving as general counsel for Boyd's association.

Then in May of that year, when Boyd appeared before congressional leaders, he found himself just one seat away from Gary Grant. While their farms were only seventy miles apart, their journeys to this point had been very different. Grant and his parents had been fighting the USDA for decades and hadn't won yet, whereas Boyd had found his way to victory. Maybe he could help others get settlements from the government, he thought.

CHAPTER FOURTEEN

———◆———

MAN BEHIND THE NAME

Tㅐㄷㄸ HERE ARE THOUSANDS OF PEOPLE WHO OWE A LOT TO PIGFORD—
myself included. While you most certainly recognize that name by
the lawsuit frequently mentioned in this book, there's an actual man
behind the case. Allow me to introduce you to Timothy Pigford.

Timothy is a fourth-generation farmer in southeastern North
Carolina. His family "came out of slavery farming,"[277] and their story
seems to have set the stage for his longtime fight for Black farmers. His
great-great-grandfather was a slave on a plantation owned by a man
named Edward Pigford in Willard, North Carolina. Once Timothy's
ancestor became a free man, he kept farming and took on the last name
Pigford. Even Timothy's first name has a connection to land: "timothy"
is defined as a tall perennial grass that is native to Europe and is used as
hay for cattle and horses.

He was born and raised in Columbus County, North Carolina, adja-
cent to where his great-great-grandfather had been a slave, in Pender

County. Timothy's dad died when he was 4. He lived on his grandfather's farm with his mother, May, and started to farm when he was 8. He learned to stand far away from their tobacco at the warehouse, as he was told "they'd downgrade our tobacco if they knew we were black."[278] He also learned that some local White farmers helped out Black farmers when his uncle would take him down the road on Monday afternoons to borrow a tractor from a White farm so he could put in the tobacco on Tuesdays.

When Timothy attended Pender High School, he served as president of the Future Farmers of America chapter. Sometime before Timothy graduated in 1969, he was recognized with a Young Farmer of the Year award. He attended the University of North Carolina Wilmington—pursuing degrees in history and political science, *Newsday* reported—but he didn't finish. He dropped out in 1973, started working at a chemical plant, and rented 25 acres, with dreams to own land once he could afford it.

"After growing up and going to college I decided I really wanted to farm again. So I asked family for help. But older Black people are scared to sign their names to something concerning land .... After the Civil War the government gave some families 40 acres and a mule and they have held onto it so dearly. Still many have been cheated out of land—their own protectiveness may have caused land to be lost,"[279] he told members of Congress in 1984. He tried explaining how wills and other protections worked to members of his family, but he still found it difficult to break through their fear. There was a freedom and power in owning land, he believed. Land was equal to independence.

The first year he applied for a loan from the Farmers Home Administration was 1973. He wanted to buy 100 acres of farmland next to a major highway for $47,000. The cost originally was $55,000 but the owner had dropped the price. Timothy trusted the Farmers Home Administration (FmHA). He thought the agency would help him buy the land. He was unaware of the hassle he was about to go through until some time later.

His farm ownership loan was approved, but with a condition. He needed to receive additional financing from the Federal Land Bank—the

FmHA would make up the difference between the bank loan and the cost of the land. The bank said it would approve it, if he put up 10 percent stock. It was a requirement on all land purchases. Timothy had recently left college so he didn't have the $4,700. He didn't have credit established either. He went back to the FmHA, thinking the agency was there to help young farmers like himself get started. Instead, the FmHA said it couldn't approve his loan and would need to terminate the application. They couldn't give him 100 percent financing. He also wasn't told about programs with reduced interest rates or other assistance that he could use to buy his farm.

When Timothy married his wife, Clara Janice, in 1975, farming was still part of the plan, along with a family. They received a $21,500 home loan from the FmHA, according to *Business North Carolina*,[280] and then moved from Pender County to a house they built in the tiny community of East Arcadia, in Bladen County.

Timothy rented more acres and grew corn and soybeans. He got a job at the Hercules chemical manufacturing plant in Wilmington, about thirty miles away from his home in an effort to save money to finally buy the farm. He planned for his sons to farm with him, and after he and his wife had two boys, they even called themselves "Pigford, Pigford, Pigford & Pigford"[281] during family meetings. "My family had been farming for four generations, and my boys were going to be the next generation, so we wanted them to learn,"[282] he explained in 1998.

By the time he found another farm to purchase, he thought he was pretty financially secure.

But again, he encountered roadblocks. Federal Loan Bank had a 10 percent stock requirement. There was no information about FmHA programs that could help. The county committee simply denied his loan. This would continue for eight years. He would get a loan to rent land, which cost more in the long run because it wasn't the best land. It didn't have "the best conservation practices or drainage. I had to build this all up, which reduced my chances over the long run of making a profit at the end of the year to pay my loan back to the Farmers Home Administration,"[283] he explained to lawmakers later.

However, it was a meeting in September 1976 that was the genesis for the decades-long legal battle that would not only result in financial, mental, and physical anguish for Timothy and his family, but would also lead to the billion-dollar settlement of the class-action lawsuit bearing his name. It was well before he was described by politicians, attorneys, and farmer advocates as persuasive, aggressive, stubborn, and tenacious, or as someone who shunned the spotlight. "Tim has never wanted the limelight," said attorney Alexander Pires, who filed the first case on behalf of Pigford and more than 400 other Black farmers before civil rights leaders Chestnut and Sanders would join him a few months later. "[Pigford] seldom gets up in front of a microphone or camera. But deep down, he's the heart of this entire movement."[284]

That September, Timothy arrived early in the town of Council—about eleven miles from his home—for his afternoon meeting with the Bladen County's Farmers Home Administration office. Timothy requested a loan to buy a 170-acre farm for $110,000. About 140 acres had been cleared. He no longer wanted to be a tenant farmer. "I was excited, and I had my heart set on buying that farm. I'd always rented, and this was going to be mine,"[285] he told *Business North Carolina*. The county supervisor asked him how much equity and equipment he had. Timothy was told he didn't have "enough equipment to properly farm and manage the farm."[286] But his plan had been to request an operating loan to purchase additional equipment if his loan to buy the farm was approved. He said they told him, "I didn't have enough sense to raise tobacco—that I'd been to college and I ought to go teach school or something."[287]

He kept farming on his rented land, but his debt grew, in part because of Mother Nature. After suffering through droughts in 1977 and 1980, he was finding it even more difficult to pay back the operating loans. Then in 1982, he said he was told he needed to increase his operation because he didn't have enough crops to carry the debt loan. He doubled his operation but didn't get the funds for a tractor to handle the larger amount of crops. He had 310 acres at that point and was using a 50-horsepower tractor. He received funding to buy a set of four-row planters, replacing the two-row planters he had. He needed an 80-horsepower tractor, but the county supervisor told him that was too big. He missed the planting deadline for the federal crop insurance, and because the markup on corn and beans is slim, he couldn't pay back his operating loan in 1983. He said he asked again for money to buy a tractor that year, but it was denied.

Timothy's appeals to diversify into hogs, tobacco, and vegetable crops—turning his farm into a full-time operation instead of one producing just corn, which had to be planted by mid- to late April, and soybeans, planted by early June—were also denied. He was discouraged by the FmHA from soil-conserving and labor-serving methods. It took about $45,000–$50,000 to put in the crops and he projected gross income of around $90,000, he later told members of Congress. He felt put off repeatedly by the FmHA. Sometimes his appointments at the office would be interrupted when the official decided to go to lunch. It got to the point where Timothy had such a nervous stomach before those meetings that he said he would want to carry in a box of Maalox, sit it on the desk, and say to the county supervisor, "Let's go at it." He often felt his blood pressure racing when he left. The response seemed to be the same every time: You can't make it in farming. You would be better off with a public job.

Every year that he requested an ownership loan to buy the property, he learned it was denied by the county committee. The reason, he thought, was racism. White farmers appeared to be getting loans. One had even gotten a 100-horsepower tractor. It was the good ol' boy network, he would later say.

More droughts came in 1983 and 1984. He couldn't get funds to buy a tractor so had to rent one. Then Hurricane Diana hit on September 13, 1984. They hadn't seen a storm this powerful since Hurricane Hazel in 1954. It was the first major hurricane to pelt the eastern U.S. in more than twenty years and caused $79 million in damage, the state estimated. The storm pummeled the 280 acres of corn and "beanland"[288] Timothy rented in Bladen and Columbus counties. He seemed to have nowhere else to turn. He had no equity. He had depreciated equipment. And he was paying around $12,000–$14,000 to rent the land. It looked like this might be the end of farming for the man upholding a four-generation tradition—the man who liked to say that he loved farming so much "there's dirt under my fingernails."[289]

Then, shortly after the storm, Timothy Pigford, the corn and soybean farmer from Bladen County, North Carolina, was invited to the nation's capital.

He traveled from his home in Riegelwood—about twenty-three miles east of Wilmington—to Washington, D.C., in the middle of the week to testify at a hearing of the House Judiciary Subcommittee on Civil & Constitutional Rights. The witnesses listed for that day were attorneys, government officials with the USDA and FmHA, lawmakers, and leaders of community housing organizations and an emergency land fund. Timothy was described as representing "concerned farmers of North and South Carolina."[290] He told the panel about his dream to own and farm his own land—and about the lack of information offered regarding programs from the Farmers Home Administration in his county. "I think it is really a disgrace that in this country, in these modern times, as the gentleman before me has said, that American soldiers, Black and White, have gone on foreign soil and fought for freedom and for the rights of other foreigners to farm their land. President Lincoln gave to Blacks after the Civil War 40 acres and a mule, and at the present rate that Blacks are losing land today, we have lost the mule and almost lost the 40 acres,"[291] he told them.

As Timothy spoke to members of Congress on September 26, 1984, he still needed money to plan for 1985. The process was complicated, with sheets of information to fill out and multiple trips to his local FmHA office to apply for loans. Instead of receiving training or technical advice, all he would hear was, "Where the hell is the payment?"[292] After registering his concerns, he also wanted—no, needed—to use the remaining time during the hearing to offer his recommendations. There were many, but a few ideas topped the list. There could be a special review or a way to oversee that each county office is giving loans out fairly. Each office could report regularly how many White and Black farmers got loans and for how much. More minority personnel could be hired. The complicated coordinated financial statement could be changed to a recordkeeping system that is "more meaningful and helpful to farmers."[293]

And, they could also investigate charges of discrimination. If the problems continued, he didn't think there would be any Black farmers by the year 2000. He believed that racism was a reason why his farm ownership loan was denied. "I feel that in 1973, if I would have been a young White guy walking into that office, I would have had that farm," he told members of Congress. "Right now that farm is probably worth twice to two-and-a-half times in value."[294] He thought he would have made it if he would have had the proper equipment and been able to purchase the land.

He was the only Black farmer to testify.

Sadly, the trip to Washington, D.C., didn't seem to alter his course; he wasn't suddenly awarded the funds he had been so desperate to receive for eight years.

In 1985, the county committee didn't just deny him an ownership loan, they denied him an operating loan too. That year was his tenth wedding anniversary. He had been farming on his rented land for a dozen years, yet he was told that he "lacked the training and experience to be a successful farmer. A county official suggested he become a teacher," *Business North Carolina* reported.[295]

Instead, he filed a discrimination complaint with the USDA. He didn't want his family's history in farming to end with him. He didn't want his sons to struggle trying to purchase farmland just as he did. Little did he know then that his financial situation was about to take an even greater turn for the worse. As his farm debt grew, the situation was again complicated by Mother Nature. There were more droughts and another major hurricane. His wife's income as a kindergarten teacher couldn't help pay all the bills. The 1998 *Business North Carolina* story said she earned $12,000 a year as a teacher's aide while he had made $14 an hour in his job at the Corning Corp. optical fiber manufacturing plant in Wilmington. In 1986, their power was cut off. They were in the dark for a year and twelve days.

And that wasn't the end of his woes. The resulting lean years caused the government to start the foreclosure process in 1992. Timothy was "by then $55,000 behind on $200,000 in loans,"[296] *Business North Carolina* reported. All his work was going to waste. What's more, the government started the process of trying to take his house. In fall 1994, he and his family were evicted. In May 1995, federal marshals seized their home. His wife's brother bought the house in an auction later that year and let them return.

Undeterred, Timothy continued to look to the future. It was time for a bold new move.

CHAPTER FIFTEEN

———————

SEEDS OF PROMISE

I N 1990, ROBERT WILLIAMS JR. WAS THE ONLY BLACK FARMER OWNING land in Nolan County, Texas, which is about fifty miles west of Abilene. When Williams purchased 349 acres, he said a Farmers Home Administration (FmHA) official told him, "You got this old farm, I helped you get in. Son, you standing up there smiling, but you're going to have to fight like hell to keep it."[297]

Over the next few years, Williams alleged, FmHA employees ridiculed him and denied him loans and assistance because of his race. Williams said White farmers in his county taunted him, and that someone killed his dogs, glued the locks on his gate shut, and hung a banner that read "KKK Go Home Nigger" at his farm's entrance.[298]

"It wasn't no secret," he told the Associated Press in 1994. "They let me know up front that I wasn't like the white man. When it came time for me to get money or do certain things, they just wouldn't do things."[299]

Bob Nash, then the USDA's undersecretary for small communities and rural development, confirmed that an agency investigation uncovered discrimination against Williams. In August 1993, Williams's lawyer, James Myart, was under the impression that he had negotiated a $1.08 million settlement for farm liabilities and damages, and more than $270,000 in legal fees. According to Myart, the acting branch chief for the FmHA's Equal Opportunity Division approved the agreement. A month later, however, the FmHA acting administrator rejected the deal. The AP reported that she "offered to take the farm to satisfy the operating loan debt and to help work out agreements with other creditors. The FmHA was willing to lease the land back to Williams with a purchase option or help find another farm."[300]

"I was a good old boy," Williams told the AP, "until I got a farm of my own."[301]

In March 1994, Williams and his wife Laverne filed a federal civil rights lawsuit against U.S. Department of Agriculture secretary Mike Espy (who was later replaced as the defendant in William's suit by Espy's successor, Daniel Glickman). More than a year later, Williams and his wife, along with three other minority farmers, filed a proposed class-action suit against Espy (and later Glickman), alleging that he and his predecessors "have developed and maintained a system of institutional racism and discrimination against American citizens on account of their race, black and brown, and national origins, African and Mexican."[302] Williams and the other plaintiffs were seeking $5 million to redress the damages caused by the FmHA. The USDA's Office of Civil Rights Enforcement confirmed that the four men and their families had been discriminated against by the FmHA.[303]

"All of them have suffered grievous financial losses, loss of credit and certainly serious emotional mental anguish," their attorney, Les Mendelsoh, told the AP. "I believe ...that Secretary Espy is very sympathetic to the plight of these minority farmers who have been discriminated against by prior administrations, but his failure to act decisively is a ratification of the past discrimination."[304]

Nash defended Espy, the first Black agriculture secretary, telling the AP, "We're the ones who found these people were discriminated against.

We found it—not the other administrations. From our standpoint, we're taking aggressive action on these cases that have been around for years. We're not just sitting on our duffs over here."[305]

In a statement, Espy said his department would do "everything we can to ensure that those who have been discriminated against are treated fairly and with justice."[306] The USDA offered to eliminate the four farmers' debt and offer them new operating loans if they needed them. Their attorney was seeking additional damages and legal fees.

The class action sought to include any persons who in the past twenty years had done business with the FmHA, participated in its direct farm ownership and loan programs, were subjected to any form of discrimination prohibited by federal law, and had suffered economic and emotional distress as a result.[307]

In February 1997, U.S. District Court Judge Thomas A. Flannery denied the plaintiffs' motion for class certification, ruling that the proposed class definition was "too overly broad and that their claims were not typical or representative of the claims of typical class members."[308] Later that year, Williams withdrew from the case and settled his claims against the USDA for less than half of the $1.4 million that was purportedly offered to him three years earlier. His attorney called it the "saddest day in my career as a lawyer and as a United States citizen."[309]

In a statement, Williams and his wife said they had "no choice but to accept the government's offer....We were faced with failing health, the loss of our farm and our home, and further ridicule in our hometown. We thought we could trust our government. We were wrong."[310]

While Williams might have failed to fully bring the U.S. Department of Agriculture to its knees for its unlawful and unjust practices, it accomplished something important. It piqued the interest of another attorney who had battled the federal government over its treatment of minority farmers. Alexander Pires, of Portuguese descent, is a former antitrust lawyer for the U.S. Department of Justice and was deputy assistant secretary of the U.S. Department of Housing and Urban Development under President Jimmy Carter. After moving to a private practice in 1981, Pires specialized in agricultural law.

"We studied that [Williams] case and tried to figure out a way to help black farmers at least in some limited way," Pires said during his testimony before a U.S. House of Representatives subcommittee on September 28, 2004. "And the Pigford case grew from the failures of the Williams case and our idea was to try to file a black farmers case that would get some relief and would get money."[311]

On August 28, 1997, Pires and a group of other attorneys from four predominantly Black law firms and four mostly White law firms filed a class-action complaint on behalf of Timothy Pickford and four hundred other African-American farmers. According to the complaint, the USDA when processing applications of African-American farmers for farm programs "willfully discriminated against them" and failed to investigate their complaints of discrimination, even though they were required to do so by the Civil Rights Act of 1964 and the Equal Credit Opportunity Act.[312]

The lawsuit alleged that when Black farmers made complaints to the USDA, the department "avoided processing and resolving the complaint by stretching the review process out over many years; conducted a meaningless, or 'ghost investigation,' or failed to take any action."[313] Remarkably, Pires received all the proof he needed in the form of comments made by Lloyd Wright, then the director of the USDA's Office of Civil Rights, in a published article in the *Richmond Times-Dispatch* in May 1997. Wright, a Black farmer himself, told the newspaper that he had only recently learned that the USDA hadn't responded to complaints of discrimination since its Office of Civil Rights had been disbanded under President Ronald Reagan in 1983.[314]

"I don't think people knew of the extent of some things that were undone that needed to be fixed," Wright told the newspaper.[315]

At the time, according to the report, the office's backlog of discrimination investigations included 540 cases. Wright's jaw-dropping admission came on the heels of a scathing 121-page study by the USDA's Civil Rights Action Team, which recommended ninety-two changes to end bias in the department. The recommendations included establishing a separate civil rights division within the USDA's general counsel office, requiring all USDA employees to undergo civil rights training annually, and setting up a new task force to provide remediation to farmers who alleged discrimination.[316] The task force noted that minority farmers had said "the federal government writes off millions of dollars in loans to foreign countries that cannot pay, yet forecloses on U.S. farmers when they cannot pay."[317]

"USDA's painful history of individual and class-action lawsuits, court orders, media exposés, numerous Congressional hearings, and reports depicts the department as a stubborn bureaucracy that refuses to provide equal opportunity to all as the law requires," reported the auditors, who also found that "minority and small farmers believe that USDA has participated in a conspiracy to take their land."[318]

Pires and the other attorneys faced one seemingly insurmountable obstacle. The U.S. Department of Justice argued that the farmers' complaints were too old and the statute of limitations to bring a lawsuit against the federal government had expired, which would have prevented about two thousand Black farmers from receiving cash compensation. The federal government also fought to try the cases separately because there were too many individual allegations to proceed with the case at once. In April 1998, Attorney General Janet Reno informed members of Congress that a statute of limitations clause that protects federal agencies did indeed require all cases more than two years old to be thrown out. It seemed that many of the Black farmers who had faced years of discrimination would be deprived of justice again.

Then in July 1998, Congress approved legislation that removed the two-year statute of limitation in federal discrimination cases. The bill, led by the Congressional Black Caucus, paved the way for the lawsuit to move forward with thousands of complainants. Politicians from both sides of the aisle, including House Speaker Newt Gingrich, helped push the initiative.

On October 9, 1998, U.S. District Court Judge Paul L. Friedman certified the case as a class-action lawsuit and defined the class as "[a]ll African-American farmers who (1) farmed between January 1, 1983, and February 21, 1997 [the timeline for filing complaints with the USDA was later expanded to January 1, 1981 through July 1, 1997) ; and (2) applied, during that time period, for participation in a federal farm program with

USDA, and as a direct result of a determination by USDA in response to said application, believed that they were discriminated against on the basis of race, and filed a written discrimination complaint with USDA in that time period."[319]

Government officials must have known they didn't have a chance to defend the U.S. Agriculture's long track record of discrimination. In January 1999, attorneys representing the Black farmers reached a tentative deal with the federal government, which proposed dividing the farmers into two groups. One group would include those who complained of discrimination involving lending and debt. For those farmers, the government would write off debts and provide them with comparable land they lost. J. L. Chestnut, a legendary Black attorney from Selma, Alabama, whose profound work I've discussed earlier, said those packages might average $200,000 per farmer. The second class would involve farmers whose claims the government were still protesting, and those cases would be decided with one-day binding arbitration, which might result in settlements of $1 million or more.[320]

Rosalind Gray, then the USDA's civil rights director, said the department wouldn't admit to having discriminated against the Black farmers but "would agree that its procedures in handling bias claims had been flawed."[321]

After little to no investigation into the Black farmers' individual claims, Friedman approved a settlement on April 14, 1999, that was estimated to total $2 billion for thousands of Black farmers.[322] Under the approved framework of the settlement, Black farmers had a choice of one of two "tracks" for being paid. Under Track A, a claimant would receive a tax-free lump sum of $50,000, plus forgiveness of their debt on USDA loans affected by discriminatory conduct. Farmers who believed they had more credible evidence of discrimination by the USDA were allowed to seek even higher awards by opting for arbitration through Track B. There was a higher standard of proof—preponderance of the evidence—for those farmers in Track B, but it also afforded them the possibility of a tailored settlement and more damages. The average debt for most Black farmers was between $75,000 to $150,000.[323]

"It's the first time ever in a racial discrimination case that serious money has been paid out," Pires said at the time. "I think it's going to encourage others to speak out."[324]

In an opinion that was attached to the consent decree, Judge Friedman opened with this eloquent summation: "Forty acres and a mule. As the Civil War drew to a close, the United States government created the Freedmen's Bureau to provide assistance to former slaves. The government promised to sell or lease to farmers parcels of unoccupied land and land that had been confiscated by the Union during the war, and it promised the loan of a federal government mule to plow that land. Some African Americans took advantage of these programs and either bought or leased parcels of land. During Reconstruction, however, President Andrew Johnson vetoed a bill to enlarge the powers and activities of the Freedmen's Bureau, and he reversed many of the policies of the Bureau. Much of the promised land that had been leased to African American farmers was taken away and returned to Confederate loyalists. For most African Americans, the promise of forty acres and a mule was never kept."[325]

In his sixty-five-page opinion, Friedman went on to write about how nonetheless, despite systemic racism and broken promises, Black farmers had persevered. By 1920, there were 925,000 African-American farms in the U.S., he noted. Friedman wrote about the establishment of the U.S. Department of Agriculture in 1862 and how it became a full cabinet department in 1889. In 1999, the USDA had an annual budget of $67.5 billion and administered loans of $2.8 billion. As the USDA grew, Friedman noted, the number of Black farmers decreased dramatically, to only 18,000 owning fewer than three million acres of land in 1999.

"The United States Department of Agriculture and the county commissioners to whom it has delegated so much power bear much of the responsibility for this dramatic decline," Friedman wrote. "The Department itself has recognized that there has always been a disconnect between what President Lincoln envisioned as the 'people's department,' serving all of the people, and the widespread belief that the Department is 'the last plantation,' a department 'perceived as playing a key role in what some see as a conspiracy to force minority and disadvantaged farmers off their land through discriminatory loan practices.'"[326]

Friedman's opinion included examples of Black farmers who complained that "county commissioners had discriminated against them for years, denying their applications, delaying the processing of their applications or approving them for insufficient amounts or with restrictive conditions."[327] He noted that in several Southeastern states, it took three times as long for a Black farmer to be approved for a loan compared to a White one. He documented the experiences of Alvin E. Steppes, a Black farmer from Lee County, Arkansas. In 1986, according to the opinion, Steppes applied to FmHA for an operating loan. Although Steppes fully complied with the application requirements, he was denied. As a result, Steppes didn't have the money to plant his crops or to pay for fertilizer and crop treatment for what he did plant, so he ended up losing his farm.[328]

Calvin Brown, a Black farmer from Brunswick County, Virginia, applied for an operating loan in January 1984, a few months before the planting season. When he inquired about the status of his loan the next month, the county supervisor told him it was being processed. When he returned a month later, the supervisor told him there was no record of his application and he had to reapply. When Brown finally received his loan in May or June 1984, planting season was over. His money was also placed in a "supervised" bank account, and he was required to obtain a supervisor's signature before withdrawing money. The opinion noted that this was "frequently required of African American farmers but not routinely imposed on white farmers."[329]

The sad stories went on and on. George Hall, an African-American, was the only farmer in Greene County, Alabama, who was denied a disaster payment for four of his crops in 1994, even though the entire county had been declared eligible. James Beverly of Nottaway County, Virginia, had been a successful pig farmer before going to the FmHA to help him expand and modernize his farm. He applied for loans to purchase breeding stock, equipment, and farrowing houses. FmHA approved his loans for breeding stock and equipment, and he was purportedly told that his application for the farrowing houses would be approved as well. He bought the livestock and equipment, and then his farrowing house application was denied. He had to sell his property to pay off his FmHA loans.

"The denial of credit and benefits has had a devastating impact on African American farmers," Friedman wrote. "The farms of many African American farmers were foreclosed upon, and they were forced out of farming. Those who managed to stay in farming often were subject to humiliation and degradation at the hands of county commissioners and were forced to stand by powerless, as white farmers received preferential treatment. As one of the plaintiffs' lawyers, Mr. J. L. Chestnut, aptly put it, African American farmers 'learned the hard way that though the rules and the law may be colorblind, people are not.'"[330]

Friedman admitted in his opinion that it was "difficult to resist the impulse to try to undo all the broken promises and years of discrimination that have led to this precipitous decline" in the number of Black farmers in the U.S.[331]

"The Court has before it a proposed settlement of a class action lawsuit that will not undo all that has been done," he wrote. "Despite that fact, however, the Court finds that the settlement is a fair resolution of the claims brought in this case and a good first step towards assuring that the kind of discrimination that has been visited on African American farmers since Reconstruction will not continue into the next century. The Court therefore will approve the settlement."[332]

CHAPTER SIXTEEN

————◆————

SECOND CHANCES

W HEN THE *PIGFORD V. GLICKMAN* LAWSUIT WAS SETTLED OUT OF court and approved by U.S. District Court Judge Paul L. Friedman on April 14, 1999, it should have been a moment of triumph for Black farmers in America. It was the first time the U.S. Department of Agriculture had been held accountable for decades of racial discrimination and inequality imposed on farmers of color, and it was the first time Black farmers would be repaid for billions of dollars in lost income and stolen land.

As advocate Gary Grant once wrote of the landmark settlement: "So a group of the least expected citizens of the United States; those who were least educated formally, and those who truly trusted their government to do right by them settled the largest civil rights claim against the government in history."[333]

The consent decree negotiated by the federal government and the Black farmers' attorneys set the timetable in motion. Initially, eligible Black farmers had just six months to file their clams. If they didn't file by October 12, 1999, a farmer would have to meet the condition of "extraordinary circumstances beyond his control" under paragraph 5(g) of the consent decree to qualify for the late-filing deadline of September 15, 2000. Friedman issued an additional order on July 14, 2000, which stipulated that no late claim petition would be accepted after September 15, 2000.

Randi Roth, the independent, court-appointed monitor, testified at a congressional subcommittee hearing on September 28, 2004, that there were about 22,000 claimants who were "given a chance to prove to a neutral third party that he or she experienced discrimination."[334] At that point, according to Roth, about 61 percent of claimants had prevailed, and about 50 percent of those who had initially been denied won on appeal. So far, she testified, about $831 million worth of relief had been distributed to more than 13,500 class members.[335]

Sounds great, right? Well, the problem is that there were another 65,950 petitions that were filed after the October 12, 1999 deadline, but prior to the September 15, 2000 cutoff. Another 7,742 came in after that latter date, according to Michael K. Lewis, the arbitrator in the Pigford case.[336] Among the more than 65,000 late filers, only 2,268 were deemed to have "extraordinary circumstances beyond his control" that caused them to miss the original deadline, according to Lewis.[337]

"The overwhelming reason provided by those whose petitions were denied was some form of lack of knowledge: unawareness of the existence of a settlement, disbelief in the settlement's legitimacy, unawareness of deadlines and filing procedures, or disbelief in the petitioner's eligibility under the settlement," Lewis said.[338]

Think about that: These folks who were so-called late-filers, who didn't even know about the case—or who didn't believe the government that had treated them so badly for so long was actually going to compensate them now—were never going to formally have a chance to air their grievances. Not all of them would have been awarded, but at least they would have had their cases heard on the merits. That's how American justice is supposed to work.

Gary Grant's mother and father didn't participate in Pigford. And he didn't feel as if the $50,000 per farmer nearly covered the real losses, which he said amounted to $1.2 billion in lost assets for Black farmers in his home state of North Carolina alone. He found that even those farmers who were eligible ran into troubles. His Black Farmers and Agriculturalists Association (BFAA) received several calls a day about the Pigford case. Half of the calls were from people who had been duped. Another Black farmers group had taken money from farmers with promises that they would help them be part of the class-action lawsuit but did nothing of the sort. Other callers were trying to get their case through in order to receive the $50,000.

But claims were being denied by the arbitrator and adjudicator, which appeared to Gary to be a "concerted effort to prevent the 'actual or real farmers' from remaining in agriculture." In a three-page letter to the chairman of the Committee on the Judiciary, written in 2003 on BFAA and The Land Loss Fund letterhead, he wrote that [the USDA] asking Black farmers to provide evidence of a "similarly situated white" farmer who received loans when they were denied, was like "asking a woman in a suit who developed breast cancer from implants to match her legal claim with a neighbor who died from taking the deadly Vioxx."[339]

Others didn't even try to pursue their piece of the settlement. Many children of Black farmers, who had seen and heard stories about how their hardworking parents and grandparents had been unable to get the loans, graduated from college and decided not to return to their rural homelands. They expected to be mistreated there and preferred to try to start anew in the cities. The tradition of passing the land to the next generation was lost. Gary's siblings, for example, became writers, teachers, and employees of large corporations—and some of the next generation became lawyers.

As the months and years wore on, and more and more claims were being denied for lack of evidence or timeliness, anger among Black farmers intensified. When Gary received calls at the BFAA, he saw first-hand that only a small percentage had filed a claim. Those who did file, had tracking numbers, but most had not yet received their payment. Other calls were from journalists, who chronicled Gary's continued bitterness for the federal government agency. "They had no intention to pay us," he told *The Birmingham News* in July 2004.[340]

"The Pigford class action has been corrupted by the USDA," he said in a 2006 story in *The Daily Herald*, the newspaper in nearby Roanoke Rapids, North Carolina.[341]

While his parents were progressive in their views about their careers and about raising their children, they likely never envisioned Gary doing what he's done. He continued to hold land lost summits and to talk to the media about his fury over the way his parents and other Black farmers had been and continued to be treated. In 2001, Matthew and Florenza Grant died within six months of each other. They never received compensation from the USDA. At the same time, many Black farmers who had cheered the Pigford settlement weren't seeing the money either. Only a fraction of the farmers who filed claims—about 40 percent, Gary estimated—had received their financial rewards by then. More than 85 percent of farmers who would be eligible never even had their claims heard on their merit.

Their land was lost. But justice for Black farmers was still possible.

"It is hard for many of us to accept that 66,000 farmers would consciously wait to file a claim that would impact their right to life, liberty, and property, knowing that they were required to do so earlier," Congressman Steve Chabot (R-Ohio), the chairman of the House of Representatives Subcommittee on the Constitution, said in his opening remarks at a hearing on the Pigford consent decree on November 18, 2004.[342]

Chabot said that further investigation by the subcommittee revealed that many farmers "failed to get any notice whatsoever or failed to understand the contents of the notice if they did receive the notice. These facts lead this Subcommittee to conclude that the notice implemented in the Pigford case was either ineffective or defective as nearly two-thirds of the putative class failed to be effectively notified of the case requirements."[343]

J. L. Chestnut, one of the lead attorneys who signed off on the consent decree, told the subcommittee that Black farmers' distrust in the federal government and their disbelief that anything tangible would happen as a result of the case, were the primary reasons for the vast number of late filers.

"Except for a core of dedicated and perennial-optimist Black farmers, no one would believe—no Black farmer would believe that a government that for 150 years had ruined them would now help them," Chestnut testified. "They would only believe that when there was something tangible and concrete, what they could see or check....Mr. Chairman, I believe if you sent your staff out tomorrow, within weeks they could find another 65,000 African-Americans who didn't file, but who now want into this lawsuit. That is the cultural disconnect. That is a far deeper problem than legal notice."[344]

Poorman-Douglas Corporation, a Portland, Oregon-based company, was contracted to develop and implement the direct mail and advertising plans of the consent decree. Jeanne C. Finegan, a Poorman-Douglas consultant and former vice president and director of Huntington Legal Advertising, testified that the company purchased one-quarter page advertisements in twenty-seven general circulation newspapers and more than 115 local African-American newspapers in eighteen states to notify potential claimants. The company purchased fifteen- and thirty-second TV commercial spots on BET and CNN in January–February 1999. It also placed half-page ads in the regional editions of *TV Guide* and the national edition of *Jet*.[345] The ads read like this:

"ATTENTION: All past or present African American Farmers, your rights may be affected by a nationwide class action lawsuit. You may be entitled to compensation and damages. You may be a potential class member if you farmed or attempted to farm between January 1, 1981 and December 31, 1996, and applied to the United States Department of Agriculture (USDA) for participation in a federal farm credit or benefit program and believe that you were discriminated against based on race. Settlement of the lawsuit has been preliminarily approved by the Court. The Deadline to Opt-Out of the Class is 120 days from date of final approval of settlement. The Deadline to file a claim is 180 days from date of final approval of settlement. The Hearing before the court for final approval is March 2, 1999. If you wish to obtain more information about this case, <u>obtain a claim package</u>, or <u>obtain a form</u> to opt-out, call toll free: 1-800-646-2873."[346]

Finegan testified that Poorman-Douglas received more than 96,000 phone calls during the claims period from January 1999 to October 1999. She called it one of the "largest, sustained call volumes in a single case in the company's history."[347] She said that by the filing deadline, Poorman-Dougas had mailed nearly 50,000 claim forms and received back almost 18,000 completed forms.

"As this Committee has heard from others, about 50 percent of the 67,000 individuals who applied to file a late claim were aware of the settlement in advance, but did not act in time," Finegan said. "As this evidence confirms, a notice program may generate interest and awareness, but it cannot make someone file."[348]

Why did so many potential claimants not act in time?

"African American farmers have faced a long history of discrimination," Finegan noted. "Many class members may have believed that even with a legitimate claim, relief would not be forthcoming. This perception may have reduced, at least initially, the desire of many class members to act. The media also tended to reaffirm this perception. If the farmer did not trust the settlement was genuine, this certainly would have affected their behavior. But as word spread that the settlement relief was being granted, class members became increasingly confident that filing a claim would not, in fact, be a waste of time. At this point, the deadline was upon them and many were unable to file in time."[349]

Many Black farmers and their advocates, whether fairly or not, blamed the attorneys who negotiated the consent decree with the federal government. Thomas Burrell, a third-generation farmer and president of the Black Farmers and Agriculturalists Association, argued that most Black farmers don't have cable TV and that many elderly Black farmers don't read, let alone subscribe to *TV Guide* or *Jet*. In his testimony at the subcommittee hearing, Burrell alleged that Black farmers were the "victims of double betrayal—first by the Department of Agriculture and then by their own lawyers."[350]

"The [Department of Justice], USDA and class counsel negotiated a settlement, the consent decree, in a back room in which there was no Black farmers present," Burrell said. "We think this was by design, not by accident or innocent oversight. We were not invited to our own demise."[351]

Among other complaints, Burrell said the DOJ, USDA, and class counsel neglected to provide direct notice to thousands of Black farmers whose names and addresses were maintained by the Farm Service Agency in St. Louis; Poorman-Douglas "did not know or completely misunderstood the communications infrastructure in America's Black communities, the churches, Black regional and local newspapers and Black radio;" and that class counsel confused many Black farmers by having "very young students fill out the claim forms and by misinforming Black farmers." One way he claimed they did this was by telling the farmers that the fast-track option for settlement (known as Track A) was automatic when in fact, there was another option (Track B) that could potentially lead to higher rewards but entailed a more rigorous review process. Burell charged that by making statements such as, "You would be a fool to opt [for B] because going Track A is like taking candy from a baby"[352] dissuaded many from pursuing larger settlements.

For many Black farmers, the Pigford settlement became another broken promise like forty acres and a mule. Phillip Haynie II was a fourth-generation farmer from Heathsville, Virginia. His great-grandfather, Rev. Robert Haynie, bought sixty acres of land on September 14, 1867, which was the first land purchased by a former slave in Northumberland County, Virginia.[353]

"I'm about to lose a part of this land that I inherited due to the discriminatory practices of the USDA," Haynie II testified. "For me and my family, spanning five generations, farming is not a job. It is a way of life."[354]

Haynie II's guest at the congressional subcommittee hearing in September 2004 was Rev. Nathaniel Jones of Gloucester, Virginia. Haynie II said Jones was the oldest living Black farmer in the U.S. "On October the twelfth, he will be ninety-nine years old." Haynie then asked, referring to one of the more inane requirements in the review and documentation part of the claims process, "How is a 99-year-old man going to go out and find 'similarly situated farmers' when everybody that farmed with him is already dead? And he does not have access to the USDA records."[355]

Haynie II then read off a litany of ways in which the *Pigford* settlement had let down Black farmers.

"[T]he settlement failed to end discrimination against Black farmers by USDA employees," he said. "The settlement has failed to prevent the loss of Black land. The settlement has failed to provide educational and financial opportunities to help young African-Americans to engage in farming. The settlement has failed to end foreclosures on Black farmers and their land. The settlement has failed to provide the injunctive relief that is outlined in the settlement. The settlement has failed to provide Black farmers with equal and fair access to land in USDA inventory."[356]

Haynie II also accused the government of low-balling complainants who pursued the Track B option—in other words, those who elected to have their cases mediated on an individual basis with the prospect of higher payouts than the $50,000 that was available to those in Track A.

"The USDA collects and analyzes a lot of good data at taxpayers' expense, but then conveniently ignores that information when estimating Track B farmers' damage," he said. "Just another example of how the Justice Department and the USDA together have twisted what was supposed to be a good faith settlement for the class into an opportunity to fight individual farmers one by one."[357]

Haynie II also noted that those farmers were faced with taking on the government without the benefit of shared expense amongst the class for things such as counsel and experts, learning for the class, and the normal discovery procedures. "And they have to fight the government without the benefit of an open and transparent process," he said.[358]

———•———

With the help of Barack Obama, then a Democratic senator from Illinois, Black farmers were given a second chance to become part of the Pigford settlement through a provision in the 2008 Farm Bill. On

February 10, 2007, Obama announced his candidacy for U.S. president in front of the Old State Capitol building in Springfield, Illinois, where Abraham Lincoln had delivered his "House Divided" speech in 1858. Obama would go on to play an integral role in getting justice for Black farmers, many of whom were the descendants of slaves that Lincoln helped free.

Obama and U.S. Senator Chuck Grassley (R-Iowa) championed the provision that allocated an additional $100 million in restitution for Black farmers who were previously denied opportunities to join the class action because they'd missed the deadline for filing. Congressman Bennie Thompson (D-Mississippi), a senior member of the Congressional Black caucus, told reporters that Black lawmakers were going to veto the farm bill unless it reopened the Pigford settlement.[359] The remaining claims were consolidated into a single case, In re Black Farmers Discrimination Litigation, which became commonly known as Pigford II. Because the farm bill provision reopened the class action to as many as 66,000 late filers, who would be entitled to at least $50,000 each, additional federal funding would be needed.

When I first read about the possibility of another round of Pigford cases in *The New York Times*, I called John Morgan, my partner and the founder of our law firm. At the time, John wasn't very interested in the case and wasn't even sure if it would result in real damages—or fees for our firm. He wanted me to focus on personal injury claims while trying to establish a satellite office in Jackson, Mississippi. After passage of the 2008 Farm Bill, I called John back to see if he had changed his mind. I'll never forget his words to me.

"You're telling Noah about the flood," he said.

CHAPTER SEVENTEEN

A FAMILIAR NAME

WHEN I ATTENDED LAW SCHOOL AT THE UNIVERSITY OF FLORIDA IN the early '90s, I would pray before I went to bed, "Lord, please let me do good, and do well at the same time." The moment I stepped into an auditorium in Memphis, Tennessee, to meet Black farmers years after I embarked on my legal career, I felt as if all those requests I sent to God were coming to fruition. I was going to be able to do good, and potentially, one day, do well.

But the Black farmers I met in Tennessee in 2008, and all the others I would eventually meet and help—didn't know me yet. They didn't know my prayer. They didn't know my background. They didn't know my abilities.

They did, however, know Mike Espy. He was the first African-American from Mississippi elected to Congress since Reconstruction. He was also a former secretary of the USDA, the first Black person to hold that role. All those people were there because they wanted to see and hear him. They arrived by the hundreds and the thousands that night and on many other nights that followed. They gathered in towns around the South for rallies and meetings we were holding to find eligible Black farmers who were denied federal loans from the USDA and who might want to join the Pigford II case.

When we were on the way from the hotel to the meeting in Memphis, I asked Mike, "Well, what do you think?" He replied, "Just watch." We pulled up to the venue, and it was a madhouse outside. People were everywhere. Some couldn't even get into the building. When we entered, I could feel the electricity in the air. The energy. The hope.

It was very much like the hope Mike gave Blacks in the South when he emerged on the political landscape two decades earlier. In 1986, Mike set a new path for Blacks in Mississippi when he was elected to the U.S. House of Representatives. He said he was inspired by his grandfather, Thomas Jefferson Huddleston Sr., whose parents were slaves and whose work included establishing the first hospital in Mississippi for Blacks, a newspaper, and a voluntary organization that provided education and more for the descendants of slaves.

Mike's grandfather lived in Yazoo City, Mississippi, where Mike was born in 1953. Yazoo City is about sixty miles from Jackson, Mississippi. Mike's father, Henry Espy, attended Tuskegee Institute in Alabama, where his teachers included George Washington Carver. His dad then worked as a USDA county agent in Crittenden County, Arkansas, "serving the state's Black farmers," as Mike described it.[360]

Mike earned his bachelor's degree in political science from Howard University in Washington, D.C., in 1975 and his Juris Doctorate, or J.D., from Santa Clara University School of Law in California in 1978. He held positions in Mississippi, including assistant state attorney general from 1984 to 1985. Mike was a rising star in the Democratic Party. Redrawn lines split his legislative district almost evenly among Black and White voters.

When he ran for office, he bridged those racial lines and focused on issues such as securing aid for family farmers, both White and Black, and ensuring rural hospitals stayed open. He appeared in front of all-White groups, at places such as the Southern Farm Bureau building in Jackson, Mississippi, and a Kiwanis Club in Greenville, Mississippi. As reported by the *Los Angeles Times*, he asked those at the Kiwanis Club event in 1986 to "picture the district's voters as the contrasting squares on a patchwork quilt, held together by 'common threads like belief in God, common threads like respect for our country and its laws.'"[361]

Mike knocked on doors and worked to register people, telling a mostly Black audience at a catfish fry sponsored by the Democratic Party in one of his district's counties, "I need you; I can't do it by myself ... Please sir, please ma'am, turn out, serve as a poll watcher or a driver or a food-fixer. The answer is in your hands."[362] Media reports described him as young, energetic, bookish, and articulate. He frequently told voters, "Stand by me, pray for me, vote for me."[363] Mike was 32 years old when he was elected to Congress in 1986, the same year civil rights leader John Lewis won his U.S. House of Representatives seat in Georgia. *The Christian Science Monitor* wrote during Mike's 1988 reelection campaign, "he has walked his tightrope surefootedly enough that the color barrier in this Deep South district appears to be washing out like a broken levee."[364] When I met him two decades later, he was down-to-earth, intelligent, well-spoken, and charismatic.

He was Barack Obama before Barack Obama.

Mike served in the U.S. House of Representatives from 1987 to 1993, when President Bill Clinton appointed him as the Secretary of Agriculture. His immediate family was not involved in farming, but Mike's father had worked for the USDA. Moreover, Mike grew up hearing stories of discrimination from Black farmers who were relatives and acquaintances, and he later heard more from farmers he met in his new leadership role.

For example, at a high school gym in August 1993, Mississippi farmer W. James Coleman remembered telling Mike about "systemic racial discrimination"[365] in the USDA. Mike heard people call the USDA "the last plantation"[366] before so he decided to see if the statistics and data backed up the anecdotal reports. He also had studied the plight of Black farmers as a congressman. What he found then was that there were no Black farmers on any local county committee—the committee that helped determine whether or not farmers received loan approval—in all of America. Those committees were elected by their peers, which were overwhelmingly White farmers. In Congress, he had proposed a law where a Black farm representative could vote in each of the counties where African-American farmers comprised 20 percent of the farm population. The bill didn't pass. He then proposed a bill to let the Secretary of Agriculture choose a Black farmer to monitor the committees. That bill didn't pass either.

As USDA head, he tried to change the culture with a mission focused on food, nutrition, conservation, and rural development. He wanted to make it "more consumer and patron friendly."[367] He created diversity panels for the department's agencies and made sure Black people were represented on them. He wanted to be certain Clinton understood that the civil rights offices should be reauthorized. Reopening those offices paved the way for the eventual Pigford settlement. But throughout this time, Mike could sense that some people were thinking he was "reforming and doing too much."[368]

Timothy Pigford considered "Espy a longtime friend of the Black farmer."[369] But before Mike could help Black farmers any more as secretary of agriculture, he had to confront and deal with a looming ethics investigation against him. He resigned on December 31, 1994, and was succeeded by Dan Glickman, who ended up being the defendant on the Pigford I class-action lawsuit.

In August 1997, Mike was indicted for bribery by independent counsel Donald C. Smaltz. He was charged with thirty-plus counts of corruption related to more than $35,000 worth of travel, gifts, and perks from companies that he regulated as secretary of agriculture. Federal law says it is illegal to give anything of value to public officials in order to curry favor with them. Although the charges had the potential to send him to prison for more than one hundred years[370] if found guilty, Mike wouldn't plead guilty to even one of the counts.

Mike's indictment, and his resignation from the USDA before that, didn't keep him from continuing his support of Black farmers. He appeared at rallies in Washington, D.C., and various Southern states alongside civil rights figures, including the Rev. Joseph Lowery, J. L.

Chestnut (whose firm represented Timothy Pigford), John Boyd Jr., and others who were trying to make sure the claims of discrimination were not ignored. Together, they also were recruiting farmers to the class-action discrimination suit. During a four-hour meeting with about sixty farmers in Memphis in 1997, Mike—who was then with a law firm in Jackson, Mississippi—told those in attendance, "You have to fight now! You can't afford to wait another 5, 6, or 7 years."[371]

Imagine the reaction in rural America, where for years and years Blacks have been mistreated. Now someone is telling them that if they collectively act, there's a chance the government will say, "Hey, we've mistreated you all this time, but now we're going to pay you." There were a bunch of Black farmers who scoffed, "That's not going to happen. It's never going to happen." Between that and the lack of ability to communicate as widely as cellphones, social media, and press coverage enables us to do today, it was difficult to get the message out to those who had experienced racial discrimination when seeking farm loans and assistance.

In September 1997, at a rally in Lafayette Square across from the White House, Espy told a crowd of about one hundred and fifty people, including farmers and minority employees of the USDA, "Discrimination is systemic, discrimination is pervasive, and discrimination is real within the Department of Agriculture."[372]

"I'm not here to condemn [Agriculture Secretary Dan Glickman] nor to condemn President Clinton," he said. "They are beginning to do the right thing. I'm just simply here to say speed it up."[373]

Mike's own case resulted in a twelve-week trial in 1998. The prosecution said it was illegal for Mike, as a federal official, to accept about $35,000 worth of gifts, such as airfare, luggage, cash, tickets to sporting events, and other perks from companies regulated by the USDA, including Tyson Foods Inc., Sun-Diamond Growers, and Quaker Oats. In December 1998, a federal jury acquitted him of all thirty corruption charges. The twelve-member jury was mostly Black, *The Washington Times* reported.[374]

"I knew it, I knew it,"[375] Mike whispered to his attorneys after hearing the verdict.

When Mike walked outside the courthouse, he said, "Each and every day I read the 27th Psalm. And it basically says that the Lord is my light and my salvation. Whom shall I fear? Certainly not Donald Smaltz."[376]

What happened to Mike at the USDA—what went down there— might have been due to his involvement with Black farmers. Could he have been framed? Possibly. Mike was and is a good guy. Without the indictment, I even thought he could have been in line to run for president.

The next year, Mike mentioned there may be another round of the Black farmers case, which he later described as a "second coming" of Pigford.[377] Sure enough, a couple of weeks later, the media reported that the 2008 Farm Bill provided for additional claims to be heard. It was rumored that there were roughly seventy thousand late-filers who would participate in Pigford II. I soon realized we were way behind other firms. Farmers groups were already working with other attorneys.

The race for clients was on.

And I was glad to have Mike on my side. We advertised him as the speaker for the Memphis event and many others—including those at convention centers in Montgomery, Alabama; Hattiesburg, Mississippi; and Pine Bluff, Arkansas. We invited people to attend these events via newspaper ads and fliers so they could hear all about the reopening of the class-action lawsuit and how it would work. I knew Mike's reputation would attract people to those meetings and I had hoped we could then start the process of signing additional claimants to the suit.

When we were at a convention center in Pine Bluff in the fall of 2008, about two hundred people heard Mike explain to them that there was an option to get restitution for being denied federal loans. He knew that many Black farmers and their descendants had not been able to participate in the first Pigford settlement or didn't get paid the $50,000 set aside per farmer because they filed their claim too late. He assured them that it wasn't their fault because they didn't know about it. "We're going to make them pay you today," Mike told them, later saying, "This is your 40 acres and a mule."[378]

Thinking back to that first rally, the one where I rented an auditorium in Memphis, the only agreement between us was, "Let's sign up these folks and let's see what happens." The auditorium held about six hundred people. We must have had two thousand people show up that night. After Mike spoke and explained the case, we handed out packets with information for folks to fill out. My role was as the deal captain.

When I came off the stage, everyone seemed to have a question or two they didn't want to ask in the open forum. As I was talking to them and answering their basic queries, I said, "Hey, let me just give you my email address and we can follow up." I'll never forget it. Someone said, "Email? Baby, we don't even have cable where I live. We don't have connections to do emails or anything like that." That was a real slap in the face and the first inkling of just how different this situation was. It was an "aha" moment—one when I realized that perhaps the other attorneys didn't have as many claimants as they thought because of the connectivity issue.

Nevertheless, the faces of those I spoke with were filled with excitement, anticipation, and hope. And while I was feeling all of the same sensations, I walked out of that Memphis auditorium that night, feeling a burden as well. Because now I was carrying the hope for all of these folks.

CHAPTER 18

———◆———

TAKING A GAMBLE

I MUST ADMIT, I WAS IN A CHALLENGING POSITION BEFORE ENLISTING Mike Espy's help. Our firm was way behind the law firms who had worked on the original Pigford case. Those firms were by then functioning as one big "megagroup" of attorneys. Their prior work not only brought them together, but it also aligned them closely with the National Black Farmers Association and John Boyd Jr. They already had a website, www.blackfarmerclaims.com, up and running, and they were using TV and other media advertising to direct potential claimants to them, all while we were just getting started.

These other firms also had something else we didn't have—the so-called 5(g) list of late filers in the original case, which included as many as 66,000 potential clients, most of whom were not likely represented by counsel yet. Since clients had to at least prove that they tried to make a claim in the original case, the names of anyone we added to the suit had to be on that list. While U.S. District Court Judge Paul L.

Friedman ruled, in December 2008, that the 5(g) list couldn't be used to contact individuals we didn't already represent, that list was still a valuable tool that could help us confirm our clients' eligibility to pursue a claim.

Not all of the firms involved in the case were in favor of class action because it would limit attorneys' fees and put them under direct jurisdiction of the court. In my mind, however, it was the best path for both the farmers and the government. Politically, it was probably the surest way to get an appropriation from Congress, and it provided the government with finality, that the cases would end once and for all. If the cases had been settled separately, the farmers might not been awarded as much money because attorneys' fees wouldn't have been capped and the cases might have not been adjudicated for several years. In a motion to Judge Friedman on April 17, 2009, we wrote that class action was the "only procedural device that can adequately protect the interests of *all* potential claimants, not just those who happen to have filed claims first or who have the luxury of representation of counsel." As the federal government made clear, "without a certified class, claimants will be pitted against each other as they each vie for a share of the $100,000,000 presently appropriated by Congress—manifestly not a result Congress intended."

Added to those hurdles was another huge challenge: Congress had only set aside $100 million for the Pigford II claims. That wasn't nearly enough money for the additional Black farmers who were seeking at least $50,000 in damages and $12,500 to cover their federal taxes. If our firm signed on clients to this case, we and our clients needed assurance that the requisite settlement monies would be there if judgements were made in their favor. We argued vociferously on the matter and anxiously awaited a reply.

Finally, on December 8, 2010, Obama, in his second year as the 44th U.S. president, signed a $1.15 billion measure to fund the Pigford II cases. When Friedman issued an order for final approval about ten months later, I was named one of the three lead class attorneys, along with Andrew Marks of Crowell & Moring in Washington, D.C., and Henry Sanders of Selma, Alabama. As you will recall, that was exactly the line-up that Hank, Mark, and I had hoped for.

President Obama called the settlement "another important step forward in addressing an unfortunate chapter in USDA's civil rights history."[379]

"This agreement will provide overdue relief and justice to African American farmers, and bring us closer to the ideals of freedom and equality that this country was founded on," Obama said in a statement.[380]

As soon as the order for final approval was issued, Mike and I, along with our team of associates, went into overdrive identifying and securing clients who were late claimants. The firms agreed to handle certain regions and we were given Mississippi, which was good because we had already done so much groundwork there. The claims period only lasted six months. Starting in mid-November 2011 through mid-May 2012, we held ninety-seven claims processing events in twenty-two states and the District of Columbia. Some of the meetings were held on the same days, so I couldn't attend all of them, though I was present for at least 70 percent of them. I didn't want to be one of the attorneys sitting in an office in Washington, D.C., filing new claims in a vacuum each day. I wanted to be a foot soldier on the ground, talking with Black farmers about their experiences.

Law school teaches aspiring lawyers about the law and how to apply it in certain cases. What it doesn't teach you, and I believe this is one of my strengths, is the ability to communicate and how to connect with clients. Early in my career, I came to understand that a client isn't simply a name on a piece of paper, it's someone's life and livelihood. I knew we owed it to the farmers to actually hit the road and go from town to town, just as the civil rights workers did during the 1960s. We traveled throughout Mississippi and other parts of the country so we could get face-to-face with the farmers. Their stories inspired me and greatly fueled my efforts on their behalf.

At a meeting in Oklahoma City, for instance, I was with paralegals and several other attorneys assisting farmers as they completed the necessary forms. I saw a young woman pushing an elderly man in a wheelchair. I didn't want the man to have wait too long, so I introduced myself and offered him help. I found out that the gentleman was the young woman's father. I asked her for his name and address. As I proceeded to ask her more questions about what types of crops he had planted in the past, she stopped me.

"No," she said.

"No?" I asked.

"No, he wants to tell his own story."

There was a kind of resolve and respect in her voice that came from having heard his compelling story herself over the years.

For the next hour or so, the elderly man told me the story of his life as a Black farmer. He spoke of the endless obstacles and discrimination he had faced, even after serving our country in the military. As I listened intently, his became the image in my mind of who I was representing. Here was someone who had sacrificed his time and was willing to risk his life for his country, yet when he returned to the farm, he was discriminated against and held back by our government. I took a photograph with him and his daughter that day. I wanted a picture of this true American hero.

Obviously, our firm was spending quite a bit of money on travel, the rental of hotel conference rooms, and other necessities. We spent more than $8 million, and I was having to pay for all of it out of the operating budget of our office in Jackson, Mississippi. The seven shareholders in that particular office were having to invest more money, and there was obviously apprehension about whether or not it was a wise decision and if they'd get their money back. I didn't have enough funds to buy commercial spots on TV for this project. But I had an idea; my thought was to "advertise" by appearing on the local news. I hired a media consultant, Ryan Julison, who booked mostly news television interviews for me and was also able to get stories published in papers around the country in advance of our meetings. I thought that was more important than doing TV commercials anyway because farmers work all day. Rarely do they have the time to watch television, unless it's the nightly news to check the weather or to catch up on pressing events.

The powers that be at Morgan & Morgan were starting to ask why we were spending so much money when we weren't guaranteed to get enough clients to justify the expenses. Apparently, lawyers for other firms were telling them, "Hey, I don't know if this is really going to amount to anything. Who knows how it's going to work out?" I was disappointed in my partners' lack of trust in my judgment and evaluation of the case. I was frustrated because I had spent time with these Black farmers and knew how important this case was. It seemed to me that this was going to be the last chance they had to be heard, obtain justice, and get restitution. Sure, there were risks involved, but I was willing to look past them. This case was too important not to follow through until the end. Farmers face grave risks all the time. Whenever they embark on a new planting season, they risk factors even more unpredictable— from floods, frost, and drought to blight. Every time they applied for a loan, they faced the risk of ridicule, outright discrimination, denial, and/ or payment that arrived too late to assure the most effective use of the money. The risk that weighed on me the most was the risk of failing them. Their time had come, and I believed in their right to justice so much that I was compelled to take the gamble. Measure by measure I would apply the best winning strategy I could. Each night, I did the math in my head. What if we get 10,000 clients? What if out of the 10,000 Black farmers who apply, only 2,500 of them are approved?

Even though I lost some sleep, I never lost faith.

Undeterred, my team and I kept working and took the show on the road. Some of our biggest turnouts were in Northern cities such as Chicago, Detroit, Indianapolis, New York, and Philadelphia. That is where many Black farmers' children had settled after leaving their rural hometowns because of the struggles and discrimination their parents had faced there. The mass exodus of Blacks from southern farmlands was known as the Great Migration.

Between the time the U.S. declared war on Germany and entered World War I in April 1917 and the stock market crash of 1929, Blacks left the South at an average of 500 per day, or more than 15,000 per month. With the "war to end all wars" all but halting the influx of White immigrants from Europe, and the Selective Service drafting four million American men into military duty, industrialized cities in the North, Midwest, and West faced a dearth of industrial laborers.

Automotive companies, munitions factories, and steel mills, among other industries, actively recruited African-American laborers from the

South during that time, promising them higher-paying jobs, equality, better lives, and more promising futures. By the end of 1930, more than 1.3 million African-Americans lived outside the South, nearly triple the population that lived there at the turn of the century.[381]

The Great Depression slowed Blacks' movement north for a while, leaving many still in the cotton states. At that time, three of four Black Americans lived in the South, with most remaining in rural areas. According to historian Ira Berlin, "Many believed the northward movement had run its course." That belief proved to be shortsighted, however, as the onset of World War II sparked a second Great Migration of Blacks out of the Deep South. More than 1.5 million Black migrants left the South for northern cities during the 1940s. The number of those moving on was equal to the total that had left in the previous three decades combined.[382]

"Black men and women also headed west as well as north, as California particularly became a magnet for migrants from Arkansas, Louisiana, and Texas," Berlin wrote in his 2010 book *The Making of African America: The Four Great Migrations*. "The wave of immigrants did not stop with the return of peace. Instead, gathering speed with time, it continued unabated for another two decades. The three million Black men and women who exited the South between 1940 and 1960 almost doubled the number who left between 1910 and 1930."[383]

This shift in demographics is why my team and I went to such far-ranging places as Long Beach, California; Dallas, Texas; Baltimore, Maryland; and Newark, New Jersey, to find them. In the end, the attorneys working the case submitted approximately 40,000 claim forms, of which 32,587 were completed and filed on time. A court-appointed neutral adjudicator and claims administrator reviewed those claims and determined there were nearly 17,000 Track A claimants who were eligible to receive $62,500 each, totaling almost $1.1 billion in awards. About 1,200 of those claimants were our clients. Friedman approved the maximum attorneys' fees allowed under the settlement agreement. Needless to say, when our share was apportioned, it was a nice payday for the Morgan Group.

When I received a text message about the court order regarding attorney fees, I had just landed in California, where I was about to begin a much anticipated vacation with my family. I remember reading the text message and telling the cab driver, "I think I just made a whole bunch of money." I had been so fixated on securing payments for the farmers, news of the firm's payday felt like a huge bonus for me.

When the case was over, I thought back to my prayer in law school. I wasn't like so many of the other law students I knew who had a sense of what they wanted to do careerwise from a very young age. But once I was there, I thought, "Well, I hope I'm not wasting my time. I hope I'm really going to do something meaningful with this." By becoming lead counsel on the Pigford II case, I certainly confirmed that I *wasn't* wasting my time and that something meaningful did indeed result from my education. We were the voices for tens of thousands of Black farmers who had never been heard. We sought justice for them. We secured equality for them. And in the end, it was definitely worth the risk.

CHAPTER NINETEEN

—◆—

I DREAM BIG

ACH MORNING, BEFORE MY DAUGHTER LEAVES OUR HOUSE, SHE
recites a poem to me:

> *"Only as high as I reach, can I grow.*
> *Only as far as I seek, can I go.*
> *Only as deep as I look, can I see.*
> *Only as big as I dream, can I be.*
> *I'm a Francis, and I dream big."*

That inspiration originally came from children's book author Karen
Ravn, and I added the last line for a personal touch. I believe you dream
big or don't dream at all; otherwise, it's a waste of sleep. I want my children to say this because I want to set the tone for their daily experiences
and not wait for society or teachers who might have other concerns
on their minds to do it. I want my kids to dream big and to *think* big.

I added the last line because I want them to understand that going forward, no matter what, their name means something, and they should put some significance to it.

That's a lesson I learned when meeting those Black farmers; they were very sure of who they were. Farmers are very definitive people. They believe what they believe, and they stick to their morals and principles. That was something that impressed with all the folks I met and in all the stories I heard. They had an indelible sense of pride in who they are. How do most of you identify who you are? A lot of times, it's by your last name. So I thought it was important to reaffirm a strong sense of identity in my children each day.

Of course, the plight of Black farmers didn't cease with the second Pigford settlement. More needed to be done to right the wrongs and to repair the harm. Politicians, government officials, attorneys, and advocates have increased their efforts in the decade since—and many continue to do so—in order to bring an end to the "historic injustice"[384] for these and other farmers.

The Pigford settlement wouldn't bring the land back but it "certainly could close the chapter,"[385] John Boyd Jr. told NPR in 2010. Boyd and others involved in the Pigford suits also increased their efforts to ensure that Hispanic, Native American, and women farmers could participate in USDA programs. Those farmers saw the Black farmers settlement as paving the way for them. In October 2010, Secretary of Agriculture Tom Vilsack announced a $760 million settlement in a class-action suit brought in 1999 by George and Marilyn Keepseagle, farmers in North Dakota, that claimed the USDA denied loan requests made by Native American farmers and ranchers.

"Native Americans have been denied equal opportunity to obtain loan applications and assistance in completing them, and the often inaccessible locations of USDA's offices have imposed obstacles to obtaining credit on Native Americans not typically encountered by other farmers and ranchers. Those Native Americans who nevertheless applied for loans received significantly fewer loans than were provided to white farmers. Further, when loans were provided, they often included onerous terms that were not imposed on white farmers,"[386] the complaint said.

In November 2010, Congress approved a $3.4 billion settlement in the *Cobell v. Salazar* case, a class-action suit brought by Elouise Cobell, a rancher and tribal elder with the Niitsítapi Blackfoot Confederacy in Montana, and four more Native Americans, on behalf of more than 300,000 Native American farmers. The class-action suit, filed on June 10, 1966, claimed mismanagement of Indian trust funds. Cobell, who died in 2011, received a Presidential Medal of Freedom posthumously in 2016.

"The Pigford settlements only begin to make up for the long and ugly history of discrimination against Black farmers and other farmers of color in the United States," Ben Jealous, then-CEO and president of the National Association for the Advancement of Colored People, wrote in 2013 in the *Philadelphia Tribune*, which was founded in 1884 and is the nation's oldest continuously published African-American newspaper. "We encourage the Department to continue to welcome farmers of color as partners and clients, and to offer them the respect they deserve and the services they still so greatly need."[387]

Garcia v. Vilsack was filed in October 2000 on behalf of Hispanic farmers who said their credit transactions and disaster benefits violated the Equal Credit Opportunity Act. *Love v. Vilsack*, filed the same month and year as the Hispanic suit, said women ranchers and farmers had experienced discrimination in their loan applications, processing, and servicing. The plaintiffs tried for a decade to have their claims heard as a class, but Hispanic and female farmers were not certified to sue as a class; they only could submit individual claims. The Pigford settlement created the template for a "two-track resolution system" that resolved cases brought by women, Hispanic, and Native American farmers, Glickman and Vilsack wrote in a commentary published in the *Chicago Tribune* in August 2020. They recognized the trailblazing Black farmers and their efforts to "pressure Congress, USDA officials and others in the executive branch to resolve these cases."[388]

During a House Agriculture Committee hearing on the state of the rural economy in February 2018, Rep. Marcia L. Fudge (D-Ohio) told Secretary of Agriculture Sonny Perdue: "…we settled Pigford for black farmers. We settled Keepseagle for Native American farmers. So it is very, very important that we don't make those same mistakes."[389]

U.S. President Joe Biden made promises to Black, Hispanic, Native American, and women farmers during his 2020 campaign. The Pigford settlement—which came to a conclusion when he was vice president in the Obama administration—brought a painful chapter to a close and the settlements "marked the beginning of a renewed commitment to supporting diversity, equity, and an internal reckoning for the USDA,"[390] his campaign website, JoeBiden.com, stated. To help advance racial equality in rural communities, Biden pledged to address inequities in agriculture.

"Black, Brown, and Native farmers have long faced barriers to growing their agricultural businesses, including unfair prices, unequal access to government support, retaliation for civil rights complaints, and outright injustice. For more than 100 years the USDA did little to alleviate the burdens of systemic inequality for Black, Brown, and Native farmers and was often the site of injustice. Over two decades ago, class action litigation was filed alleging longstanding discrimination against Black, Latino, Native, and women farmers. The cases dragged on for many years without relief for the complaints and impacted farmers struggled to regain the footing they lost before and during the litigation," his website stated.

In early 2021, in the midst of news about the coronavirus pandemic, the Capitol riot, the economy, Biden's presidency, and Kamala Harris making history as the first female and first woman of color to become vice president, headlines also reflected the plight that Black farmers still face—and the hope they maintain that the next generation could be successful and thrive. "For Black Farmers, Old Wounds Still Sting," wrote *The Washington Post*. In *Politico*, "Black farmers look to next Congress, Biden to dismantle 'culture of discrimination.'" And in *The New York Times*, "Two Biden Priorities, Climate and Inequality, Meet on Black-Owned Farms." That latter story noted that Biden "has pledged to tackle a legacy of discrimination that has driven generations of Black Americans from their farms, with steps to improve Black and other minority farmers' access to land, loans and other assistance, including 'climate smart' production."[391]

At the same time, his pick for Secretary of Agriculture was Vilsack—a name recognizable on the second class-action suit because of his position as head of the USDA and because he had received some of the blame for how the USDA mishandled issues. Although media outlets reported in December that Biden met with organizations that help Black farmers, some folks have criticized Biden's choice. Among the critics is Boyd, who said he told Biden on a call that the USDA needs "new blood and new leadership ... We need people that are sensitive to the needs of Black and other small scale farmers—Native American farmers, women, Hispanics—and [we need to] make sure that we are part of USDA."[392]

Legislation before Congress in 2021—co-sponsored by three senators who ran for the 2020 Democratic presidential nomination—was "aimed at addressing and correcting historic discrimination within the U.S. Department of Agriculture in federal farm assistance and lending that has caused Black farmers to lose millions of acres of farmland and robbed Black farmers and their families of hundreds of billions of dollars of inter-generational wealth."[393] The Justice for Black Farmers Act—the legislation introduced in November 2020 by Sens. Cory Booker (D-N.J.), Elizabeth Warren (D-Mass.), and Kirsten Gillibrand (D-N.Y.)—aims to "once and for all end discrimination within" the USDA and to help fight Black land loss with grants and protections of property rights. The changes within the USDA would include establishing an independent civil rights oversight board to conduct reviews of civil rights complaints appeals, to investigate discrimination reports, and to provide oversight to the county committees in the Farm Service Agency. Changes would also include an Equity Commission that would work to reform those county committees.

Efforts to address systemic racism come as the number of Black farmers, in particular, remains on the decline in the U.S. Booker, the lead sponsor on the bill, pointed out the "direct connection between discriminatory policies within the USDA and the enormous land loss we have seen among Black farmers over the past century."[394] In 1920, the 925,710 Black farmers in the U.S. represented 14 percent of all farms. In 2017, there were about 48,700 Black "producers" in America—representing 1.4 percent of the nearly 3.4 million producers in the U.S.— according to the data from the USDA's 2017 Census of Agriculture. Only 7 percent of Black-operated farms had sales and government payments of $50,000 or more in 2017. Black-owned farms number 35,470. Groups such as the Black Farmers & Agriculturalists Association have continued to hold Black land loss summits that addressed land acquisition, farming research, inheritance practices, and creative solutions to be successful. Other groups, such as Georgia-based New Communities and Southeastern African-American Farmers Organic Network, continue to help farmers.

The proposed act would address "heirs property" issues with more funding authorization from a program created in the 2018 Farm Bill. The senators hope to give Black farmers grants and access to USDA operating loans for up to 160 acres of farmland. According to the USDA's 2017 Census of Agriculture, Black-operated farms are, on average, 132 acres. Advocates of the bill say they believe that these changes, if approved, will help make farming more inclusive and equitable. In announcing the legislation, the sponsors also said the act would "forgive USDA debt of Black farmers who filed claims in the Pigford litigation."[395]

I'm still working to help Black farmers too. After all of the Pigford II claims were paid, there was about $9.5 million left in the money the federal government had appropriated. The money can't be returned, and we couldn't give more to the Black farmers because they would have received a greater amount than the claimants in the original case, so the money went into what is called a *cy pres* fund. That money can be distributed to organizations that help further class members' rights. With the help of Farm Aid, Inc., we identified twenty-six groups that worked to advance the cause of minority farmers. Some of our biggest beneficiaries were the Arkansas Land and Farm Development Corporation, Federation of Southern Cooperatives, National Black Farmers Association, Oklahoma Black

Historical Research Project, and the Southwest Georgia Project. The latter organization, founded by Charles and Shirley Sherrod, has worked to address Black land loss, voter rights, school integration, and other civil rights issues since 1961. We met with Black farmers and advocates in Atlanta to decide what to do with the remaining money, and we're still working through plans to seed some type of financial institution that can loan money to Black farmers when they can't otherwise find funding.

I'm also working to make sure that underdogs like Black farmers will have voices to speak for them and advocates to defend them in the future. Along with fellow University of Florida Levin College of Law graduates Yolanda Cash Jackson and Paul Perkins, I've helped endow five scholarships at the UF School of Law for graduates of historically Black colleges and universities. Florida now has one of the top ten law schools in the entire country and it's highly competitive. Obviously, you can't compete if you don't have the finances to help you through. I wanted to give back to the University of Florida for the education I received there, but I wanted to make sure my gift was geared toward students whose experiences closely mirrored mine in terms of going to college and law school. The Black farmers I represented produce food and many times don't know where it's going or whom it will feed. I don't know who is going to receive these scholarships in the future; I only know that we're planting seeds that will increase the number of Black lawyers in Florida.

Additionally, I am launching the Greg Francis Just Harvest Foundation, which has three core principles—family and identity, education, and entrepreneurialism. Initially, our emphasis will be on helping Black communities, hoping to plant seeds that will grow in each of the aforementioned areas, seeds of justice if you will. I want to encourage others to use the Bible as an educational tool for building character and a sense of strength. I want to create a platform in which other investors can learn and reap the fruits and benefits of investing into Black businesses and communities. I plan to use the stories of Black farmers to show how successful they were before government handouts and loans muddied the water. I want to promote private investment into similar areas of Black entrepreneurialism and make certain that the Black farmers' stories are heard so we can inspire others like them.

In 2018, I left Morgan & Morgan and joined my longtime friend Joseph A. Osborne. We formed our own firm, Osborne & Francis, PLLC, which has offices in Boca Raton, Florida, and Orlando, Florida. If you remember, he was the attorney who hired me for my first summer clerkship at Bobo, Spicer, Fulford, et al. Joe is an exceptional attorney in his own right, helping secure millions of dollars in settlements in medical device and pharmaceutical class action lawsuits. We represent a number of municipalities in Florida and Kentucky in their efforts to hold pharmaceutical companies responsible for the opioid crisis that has ravaged our country.

Looking back, I think the Pigford settlements were a big step in the right direction in terms of righting the wrongs against Black farmers. From time to time, I still hear stories about folks who believe they're not getting the proper access to funding or assistance from the USDA. However, it's not as prevalent as it once was. I think there certainly was an acknowledgement from the USDA that they should have been doing more in the past, but I don't think Pigford was the ultimate solution. There's still much that needs to be done to correct wrongs and to ensure that they don't happen in the future.

In commentary in the *Chicago Tribune* written in August 2020, months before Vilsack was reappointed by President Biden to the position as Agriculture Secretary, he and former Secretary of Agriculture Dan Glickman stated, "The legacy of slavery agriculture shattered the ambitions and dreams and trampled the rights of Black, Hispanic and Native American farmers, sowing seeds of today's racial animus. But as the country became less rural, their plight was eclipsed by the attention given to the civil rights movement flourishing in urban America. And reports from the U.S. Commission on Civil Rights (in 1965 and 1982) of structural racism in USDA's farm programs generated little remedial action; the majority of American agriculture likewise turned a blind eye to the plight of Black farmers."[396]

The Pigford suits brought the plight of generations of Black farmers into the light. The civil rights settlements they presided over and the policies they implemented were "not perfect," the two USDA chiefs said, but they took action and learned lessons. Hopefully, for Black, Hispanic, Native American, and female farmers, they will not be ignored or forgotten. Those farmers can't afford it; the country can't afford it. Glickman and Vilsack described "addressing the vestiges of historic racism in our agricultural past" as a requirement of the job as leaders of what President Abraham Lincoln in 1862 called "The People's Department."

I hope they're sincere in addressing racism and inequality for Black farmers. At least that's my dream, and I dream big.

ENDNOTES

1   Preface: 50 Years of Courage Cooperation Commitment & Community (The Federation of Southern Cooperatives Land Assistance Fund)

2   Abril Castro and Zoe Willingham, "Progressive Governance Can Turn the Tide for Black Farmers," Center for American Progress, April 3, 2019, https://www.americanprogress.org/issues/economy/reports/2019/04/03/467892/progressive-governance-can-turn-tide-black-farmers/.

3   Castro and Willingham.

4   Panama Canal Museum, "Interesting Facts About the Panama Canal," Panama Canal Museum, accessed February 13, 2021, https://cms.uflib.ufl.edu/pcm/facts.aspx.

5   Caroline Lieffers, "The Panama Canal's Forgotten Casualties," The Conversation, April 16, 2018, https://theconversation.com/the-panama-canals-forgotten-casualties-93536.

6   Ralph Emmett Avery and William C. Haskins, *Greatest Engineering Feat in the World at Panama: Authentic and Complete Story of the Building and Operation of the Great Waterway—the Eighth Wonder of the World* (Charleston, SC: Nabu Press, 2010), 54.

7   Avery and Haskins, 54.

8   Charles D. Ameringer, "Bunau-Varilla, Russia, and the Panama Canal," Journal of Interamerican Studies and World Affairs 12, no. 3 (1970): 328-38, January 2, 2018, https://www.cambridge.

org/core/journals/journal-of-interamerican-studies-and-world-af-fairs/article/abs/bunauvarilla-russia-and-the-panama-canal/E542357D265A143AC8A4DFB97CB83224.

9 Lieffers, "The Panama Canal's Forgotten Casualties."

10 Lieffers, "The Panama Canal's Forgotten Casualties."

11 Avery and Haskins, *Greatest Engineering Feat in the World at Panama*, 97.

12 Lieffers, "The Panama Canal's Forgotten Casualties."

13 Panama Canal Authority, "Frequently Asked Questions," PanCanal.com, accessed February 13, 2021, https://www.pancanal.com/eng/general/canal-faqs/index.html.

14 Panama Canal Authority, "History—British History in Depth: Panama Canal Gallery," BBC, February 17, 2011, http://www.bbc.co.uk/history/british/victorians/panama_gallery_04.shtml.

15 Bert Wilkinson, "Barbadians and the Panama Canal," *New York Amsterdam News*, June 30, 2016, http://amsterdamnews.com/news/2016/jun/30/barbadians-and-panama-canal/.

16 Kate Dailey, "Who on Earth Are the Zonians?," BBC News, August 11, 2014, https://www.bbc.com/news/magazine-28594016.

17 Drew Reed, "Story of Cities #16: How the US-Run Canal Zone Divided Panama for a Century," *The Guardian*, April 6, 2016, https://www.theguardian.com/cities/2016/apr/06/story-cities-16-panama-canal-zone-history-us-run-divided-city.

18 Soumyajit Dasgupta, "How the Water Locks of Panama Canal Work?," *Marine Insight*, updated February 5, 2021, https://www.marineinsight.com/guidelines/how-the-water-locks-of-panama-canal-work/.

19 Lamar Salter, "Watch This Amazing Time-Lapse Showing How Ships Get through the Panama Canal," Business Insider, October 23, 2017, https://www.businessinsider.com/this-amazing-time-lapse-shows-how-ships-get-through-the-panama-canal-gatun-lakes-2017-10.

20 "Your Town," The Panama Canal Review, February 6, 1953, 8.

21 William H. McRaven, *Make Your Bed: Little Things That Can Change*

Your Life…and Maybe the World (London: Michael Joseph, 2017), 9.

22 John Morgan, *You Can't Teach Hungry…Creating the Multimillion Dollar Law Firm* (Trial Guides, LLC, 2011).

23 Christopher Boyd, "Morgan, Colling & Gilbert Breaks Up," Orlando Sentinel, February 24, 2005, https://www.orlandosentinel.com/news/os-xpm-2005-02-24-0502240071-story.html.

24 Terry Gross, "'Black In Selma' Author Reflects On the Long March Toward Civil Rights," NPR, *Fresh Air*, July 20, 2020, https://www.npr.org/2020/07/20/893011932/black-in-selma-author-reflects-on-the-long-march-toward-civil-rights.

25 Gross.

26 Gross.

27 Federation of Southern Cooperatives/Land Assistance Fund 2005 22nd Annual Farmer's Conference in Albany, Georgia, "Overview, Problems and Suggested Remedies for the Pigford Case," press release, March 15, 2005, http://jlchestnutjrfoundation.org/PressRelease.pdf.

28 Alvin Benn, "Sanders Family Leads Alabama's Largest Black Law Firm," *Montgomery Advertiser*, February 18, 2017, https://www.montgomeryadvertiser.com/story/news/local/community/2017/02/18/sanders-family-leads-alabamas-largest-black-law-firm/98065832/.

29 Hank Sanders, "Hank Sanders: 55 Years and Still Struggling for the Full Right to Vote," editorial, Wave 3 News, October 28, 2020, https://www.wave3.com/2020/10/28/hank-sanders-years-still-struggling-full-right-vote/.

30 Heather Gray, "Interview with Alabama Attorney Hank Sanders about the Black Farmer Lawsuit Against the US Government," interview, Justice Initiative International, May 2, 2018, https://justiceinitiativeinternational.wordpress.com/2018/05/02/interview-with-alabama-attorney-hank-sanders-about-the-black-farmer-lawsuit-against-the-us-government/.

31 Gray.

32 Gray.

33 Gray.

34 Gray.

35 Gray.

36 Gray.

37 Federation of Southern Cooperatives, press release.

38 Debbie Weingarten, "The Case for Reparations for Black Farmers," TalkPoverty.org, May 1, 2019, https://talkpoverty.org/2019/05/01/ case-reparations-black-farmers/.

39 Federation of Southern Cooperatives, press release.

40 Melissa Harris-Perry et al., " 'The Melissa Harris-Perry Show' for May 4, 2013," MSNBC, May 4, 2013, https://www.nbcnews.com/id/ wbna51789265.

41 Melissa Harris-Perry.

42 Bruce Weber, "J. L. Chestnut Jr., Early Leader in Civil Rights Movement, Is Dead at 77," *The New York Times, September 30, 2008, https:// www.nytimes.com/2008/10/01/us/01chestnut.html#:~:text=Chestnut%20was%20an%20underpublicized%20figure,establishment%20 to%20achieve%20just%20ends.*

43 Staff Reports, "Once Legal Allies Now Battle in Court," *Selma Times-Journal,* October 28, 2013, https://www.selmatimesjournal. com/2013/10/28/once-legal-allies-now-battle-in-court/.

44 Martha McCartney, "Virginia's First Africans," *Encyclopedia Virginia,* October 8, 2019, https://www.encyclopediavirginia.org/virginia_s_ first_africans.

45 McCartney.

46 McCartney.

47 Mary Elliott and Jazmine Hughes, "Four Hundred Years After Enslaved Africans were First Brought to Virginia, Most Americans Still Don't Know the Full Story of Slavery," *The New York Times Magazine,* August 19, 2019, https://www.nytimes.com/interactive/2019/08/19/ magazine/history-slavery-smithsonian.html.

48 Mary Caroline Crawford, *In the Days of the Pilgrim Fathers* (Boston, MA: Little, Brown and Company, 1920), 116–117.

49 Crawford, 117.

50 Crawford, 118.

51 Elliott and Hughes "Four Hundred Years."

52 Rosemarie Zagarri, "Slavery in Colonial British North America," Teachinghistory.org, accessed February 14, 2021, https://teachinghistory.org/history-content/ask-a-historian/25577.

53 Allison T. Williams, "Cotton Was Once King of South," *Daily Press*, December 15, 2012, https://www.dailypress.com/news/isle-of-wight/dp-nws-cotton-history-sidebar-20121215-story.html.

54 Andrew Glass, "Congress Votes to Ban Slave Importation, March 2, 1807," *POLITICO*, March 2, 2018, https://www.politico.com/story/2018/03/02/congress-votes-to-ban-slave-importation-march-2-1807-430820.

55 Glass.

56 Elliott and Hughes, "Four Hundred Years."

57 Dan Allosso, "Slavery and King Cotton," *US History I: Precolonial to Gilded Age*, Minnesota Libraries Publishing Project, accessed February 14, 2021, https://mlpp.pressbooks.pub/ushistory1/chapter/slavery-king-cotton/.

58 Elliott and Hughes, "Four Hundred Years."

59 Allosso, "Slavery and King Cotton."

60 Sven Beckert, "Empire of Cotton," *The Atlantic*, December 12, 2014, https://www.theatlantic.com/business/archive/2014/12/empire-of-cotton/383660/.

61 Beckert.

62 Beckert.

63 Elliott and Hughes, "Four Hundred Years."

64 "Fort Monroe and the 'Contrabands of War' (U.S. National Park Service)," National Parks Service (U.S. Department of the Interior), accessed December 16, 2020, https://www.nps.gov/articles/fort-monroe-and-the-contrabands-of-war.htm.

65 Michael Fellman, "The First Emancipation Proclamation," *The New York Times*, August 30, 2011, https://opinionator.blogs.nytimes.com/2011/08/29/the-first-emancipation-proclamation/.

66 65 *The New York Times, Disunion: Modern Historians Revisit and Reconsider the Civil War from Lincoln's Election to the Emancipation*

Proclamation, ed. Ted Widmer (New York: Black Dog & Leventhal Publ., 2013).

67 National Park Service editors, "David Hunter," National Parks Service, U.S. Department of the Interior, September 21, 2016, https://www.nps.gov/fopu/learn/historyculture/david-hunter.htm.

68 Abraham Lincoln, "The Emancipation Proclamation," National Archives and Records Administration, April 17, 2019, https://www.archives.gov/exhibits/featured-documents/emancipation-proclamation#:~:text=President%20Abraham%20Lincoln%20issued%20the,and%20henceforward%20shall%20be%20free.%22.

69 "The Confiscation Acts of 1861 and 1862," United States Senate Historical Office, accessed February 14, 2021, https://www.senate.gov/artandhistory/history/common/generic/ConfiscationActs.htm.

70 Guy Gugliotta, "New Estimate Raises Civil War Death Toll," *The New York Times*, April 2, 2012, https://www.nytimes.com/2012/04/03/science/civil-war-toll-up-by-20-percent-in-new-estimate.html.

71 "The Senate Passes the Thirteenth Amendment," United States Senate Historical Office, accessed February 14, 2021, https://www.senate.gov/artandhistory/history/minute/Senate_Passes_the_Thirteenth_Amendment.htm.

72 Ira Berlin et al., *Free at Last: A Documentary History of Slavery, Freedom, and the Civil War* (1993; repr., New York: New Press, 2007), 314.

73 Sarah McCammon, "The Story Behind '40 Acres And A Mule'," NPR, January 12, 2015, https://www.npr.org/sections/codeswitch/2015/01/12/376781165/the-story-behind-40-acres-and-a-mule.

74 Ira Berlin, *Freedom: Volume 2, Series 1: The Wartime Genesis of Free Labor: The Upper South* (Cambridge, NY: Cambridge University Press, 1993), 338.

75 Claude F. Oubre and Katherine C. Mooney, *Forty Acres and a Mule: The Freedmen's Bureau and Black Land Ownership* (Baton Rouge, LA: Louisiana State University Press, 2012), 3.

76 Oubre and Mooney, 5-6.

77 Oubre and Mooney, 6.

78 Juan Williams, "'Black Farmers in America'," NPR, February 22, 2005, https://www.npr.org/2005/02/22/5228987/black-farmers-in-america.

79 Henry Louis Gates Jr., "The Truth Behind '40 Acres and a Mule'," PBS, September 18, 2013, https://www.pbs.org/wnet/african-americans-many-rivers-to-cross/history/the-truth-behind-40-acres-and-a-mule/.

80 Robert C. Lieberman, "The Freedmen's Bureau and the Politics of Institutional Structure," *Social Science History* 18, no. 3 (1994): 405–37, https://www.jstor.org/stable/1171498?origin=crossref&seq=1.

81 Williams, "Black Farmers in America."

82 Oubre and Mooney, *Forty Acres and a Mule*, iii.

83 "Mississippi Black Codes (1865)," Facing History and Ourselves, accessed February 14, 2021, https://www.facinghistory.org/reconstruction-era/mississippi-black-codes-1865.

84 Lowcountry Digital History Initiative, "South Carolina's 'Black Code'," After Slavery: Educator Resources, accessed February 14, 2021, http://ldhi.library.cofc.edu/exhibits/show/after_slavery_educator/unit_three_documents/document_eight.

85 Lowcountry Digital History Initiative.

86 Thomas J. Little, "The South Carolina Slave Laws Reconsidered, 1670–1700," *The South Carolina Historical Magazine* 94, no. 2 (April 1993): 86–101, http://www.jstor.org/stable/27569914.

87 "The Southern 'Black Codes' of 1865–66," Constitutional Rights Foundation, accessed February 14, 2021, https://www.crf-usa.org/brown-v-board-50th-anniversary/southern-black-codes.html.

88 Oubre and Mooney, *Forty Acres and a Mule*, v.

89 Rick Beard, "A Promise Betrayed: Reconstruction Policies Prevented Freedmen from Realizing the American Dream," HistoryNet, June 2017, https://www.historynet.com/a-promise-betrayed.htm.

90 Beard.

91 Beard.

92 History.com Editors, "Homestead Act," History.com, August 15,

2019, https://www.history.com/topics/american-civil-war/home-stead-act.

93 Oubre and Mooney, *Forty Acres and a Mule*, vi.

94 Oubre and Mooney, 13.

95 Herbert G. Ruffin II, "Davis Bend, Mississippi (1865–1887)," January 17, 2007, https://www.blackpast.org/african-american-history/davis-bend-mississippi-1865-1887/.

96 Neil R. McMillen, "Isaiah T. Montgomery, 1847–1924 (Part I)," *Mississippi History Now*, February 2007, http://www.mshistorynow.mdah.ms.gov/articles/55/isaiah-t-montgomery-1847-1924-part-I.

97 U. S. President Andrew Johnson, "December 25, 1868.—Granting full pardon and amnesty to all persons engaged in the late rebellion. By the President of the United States of America. A proclamation," Library of Congress, 1868, https://www.loc.gov/item/rbpe.23602600/.

98 Williams, "Black Farmers in America."

99 Beard, "A Promise Betrayed."

100 Carrie Kinsey, "Records of Rights: Sister Tries to Save her Kidnapped Brother, 1903," National Archives, General Records of the Department of Justice, http://recordsofrights.org/records/279/sister-tries-to-save-her-kidnapped-brother/1.

101 Douglas A. Blackmon, *Slavery by Another Name: The Re-Enslavement of Black Americans from the Civil War to World War II* (London: Icon, 2012), 252.

102 Blackmon, 249.

103 Blackmon, 250.

104 Douglas A. Blackmon, "America's Twentieth-Century Slavery," *Washington Monthly*, January/February 2013, https://washingtonmonthly.com/magazine/janfeb-2013/americas-twentieth-century-slavery/.

105 Blackmon, 430-431.

106 William Andrew Todd, "Convict Lease System," New Georgia Encyclopedia, December 12, 2005, https://www.georgiaencyclopedia.org/articles/history-archaeology/convict-lease-system.

107 Todd.

108 Mary Ellen Curtin, "Convict-Lease System," Encyclopedia of Alabama, updated May 13, 2019, http://encyclopediaofalabama.org/article/h-1346.

109 Curtin.

110 John Dittmer, *Black Georgia in the Progressive Era: 1900–1920* (Urbana, IL: University of Illinois Press, 1980), 72.

111 Dittmer, 72.

112 Dittmer, 72.

113 Dittmer, 72.

114 Dittmer, 72.

115 "Indicted for Peonage: Prominent Georgians Charged with Forcing Negroes into Servitude," *The New York Times*, November 24, 1903, 2, https://www.nytimes.com/1903/11/24/archives/indicted-for-peonage-prominent-georgians-charged-with-forcing.html.

116 Blackmon, *Slavery by Another Name*, 250–251.

117 "Georgians Fined On Peonage Charge," *Coosa River News*, December 4, 1903, 15.

118 Dittmer, *Black Georgia in the Progressive Era*, 74.

119 "Alabama Labor Law Declared to Be Invalid," *Atlanta Constitution*, December 1, 1914, 7.

120 Walter White, *Rope and Faggot: A Biography of Judge Lynch* (Notre Dame, IN: University of Notre Dame Press, 2002).

121 "Says Negroes Made Victims," *Jackson Daily News*, January 14, 1921, 1.

122 Marion Kendrick, "Stage Set for Legal Battle in 'Death Farm Case' Tuesday," *Atlanta Constitution*, April 3, 1921, 1.

123 Kendrick, 1.

124 Kendrick, 1.

125 Kendrick, 1.

126 Kendrick, 1.

127 Kendrick, 1.

128 "More Murders May Be Found," *Bamberg Herald*, Historical Newspapers of South Carolina, University of South Carolina Libraries, April 21, 1921, 1, https://historicnewspapers.sc.edu/lccn/

sn86063790/1921-04-21/ed-1/seq-1/ocr/.

129 Kendrick, "Stage Set for Legal Battle," 1.

130 Marion Kendrick, "Son of John Williams, Hero of Somme Retreat, Says Father Is Innocent," *Atlanta Constitution*, March 31, 1921, 1.

131 Rowland Thomas, "Will Come Clear on Second Trial, Asserts Planter," *Atlanta Constitution*, April 10, 1921, 1–2.

132 Thomas, 2.

133 "Charge Two Men with Murder of Eleven Negroes," *Fort Lauderdale News*, February 15, 1927, 1.

134 Thomas, "Will Come Clear," 2.

135 David L. Jordan and Robert L. Jenkins, *David L. Jordan: From the Mississippi Cotton Fields to the State Senate, a Memoir* (Jackson, MS: University Press of Mississippi, 2014), 27.

136 Jordan and Jenkins, 26.

137 Jordan and Jenkins, 29–30.

138 Jordan and Jenkins, 30.

139 Jordan and Jenkins, 27.

140 Jordan and Jenkins, 32.

141 Matthew Reonas, "Sharecropping," 64 Parishes, accessed February 15, 2021, https://64parishes.org/entry/sharecropping.

142 Reonas.

143 David E. Conrad, "Tenant Farming and Sharecropping," *The Encyclopedia of Oklahoma History and Culture*, accessed February 15, 2021, https://www.okhistory.org/publications/enc/entry.php?entry=TE009.

144 Jack Temple Kirby, "Black and White in the Rural South, 1915–1954," *Agricultural History* 58, no. 3 (July 1984): 411–22, accessed January 5, 2021, http://www.jstor.org/stable/3743088.

145 "Thomas Green Clemson," Clemson University, South Carolina, accessed February 15, 2021, https://www.clemson.edu/about/history/bios/thomas-g-clemson.html.

146 "Agreement with Sharecroppers, 1868," *Enslaved People in the Southeast*, accessed February 15, 2021, https://aserlsharedenslavedpeople.omeka.net/exhibits/show/enslaved-people-in-the-se/item/3.

147 Adam Parker, "'Call My Name': Clemson University Professor Seeks

to Credit Black Laborers on Campus," *Post and Courier*, December 25, 2019, https://www.postandcourier.com/news/local_state_news/call-my-name-clemson-university-professor-seeks-to-credit-black-laborers-on-campus/article_7f579968-1dbe-11ea-80e2-0b6b3fda7db4.html.

148 "Agreement with Sharecroppers, 1868."

149 "Agreement with Sharecroppers, 1868."

150 "Agreement with Sharecroppers, 1868."

151 "Thomas Green Clemson."

152 "Oral History Interview with William Gordon, January 19, 1991. Interview A-0364. Southern Oral History Program Collection (#4007)," Southern Oral History Program Collection, Southern Historical Collection, Wilson Library, University of North Carolina at Chapel Hill, accessed February 15, 2021, https://docsouth.unc.edu/sohp/A-0364/menu.html.

153 Jane Maguire, "Ed: A Black Sharecropper's Story," *American Heritage* 27, no. 2 (February 1976), https://www.americanheritage.com/content/february-1976.

154 Maguire.

155 Maguire.

156 Maguire.

157 Bernice Kelly Harris, "Jim Parker Hopes Ahead," Federal Writers' Project papers #3709, Southern Historical Collection, The Wilson Library, University of North Carolina at Chapel Hill, June 7, 1993, https://finding-aids.lib.unc.edu/03709/#d1e8855.

158 Lorena Hickok et al., *One Third of a Nation: Lorena Hickok Reports on the Great Depression* (Urbana, IL: University of Illinois Press, 1983), 158.

159 H. C. M. Case, "Farm Debt Adjustment during the Early 1930s," *Agricultural History* 34, no. 4 (October 1960): 173–81, http://www.jstor.org/stable/3741110.

160 Anthony J. Badger, *The New Deal: The Depression Years, 1933–1940* (Chicago, IL: Ivan R. Dee, 2002), 15.

161 "History of the Boll Weevil in the United States," Mississippi Boll

Weevil Management Corporation, accessed February 15, 2021, http://bollweevil.ext.msstate.edu/history.html.

162 Chris Dobbs, "Agricultural Adjustment Act," New Georgia Encyclopedia, updated December 14, 2020, https://www.georgiaencyclopedia. org/articles/business-economy/agricultural-adjustment-act.

163 Kenneth E. Phillips and Janet Roberts, "Cotton," Encyclopedia of Alabama, updated November 28, 2018, http://encyclopediaofalabama. org/article/h-1491.

164 Dobbs.

165 Badger, *The New Deal*, 15.

166 Hossein Ayazi and Elsadig Elsheikh, "The US Farm Bill: Corporate Power and Structural Racialization in the US Food System" (Berkeley, CA: Haas Institute for a Fair and Inclusive Society, 2015), 23, https://escholarship.org/uc/item/55v6q06x .

167 "The Dust Bowl," National Drought Mitigation Center, University of Nebraska, accessed February 15, 2021, https://drought.unl.edu/dustbowl/Home.aspx.

168 Maguire, "Ed: A Black Sharecropper's Story."

169 Peter Liebhold, "These Tractors Show 150 Years of Farming History," National Museum of American History, March 1, 2018, https:// americanhistory.si.edu/tractor.

170 Maguire, "Ed: A Black Sharecropper's Story."

171 Maguire.

172 fdr4freedoms.org editors, "Hope, Recovery, Reform: *The Great Depression and FDR's New Deal* 1933–1939," accessed February 15, 2021, https://fdr4freedoms.org/hope-recovery-reform/.

173 "Cotton Acreage Reduction Campaign Is Called Great Effort to Aid Producers," *The Town Talk*, January 11, 1934, 10.

174 "Agricultural Adjustment Act," Encyclopedia of Arkansas, updated April 4, 2009, https://encyclopediaofarkansas.net/entries/agricultural-adjustment-act-5206/.

175 F. F. R. "The Agricultural Adjustment Act of 1938," *Virginia Law Review* 24, no. 8 (June 1938): 914–19, https://www.jstor.org/stable/1068087?seq=1.

176 United States Congress Committee, *Economic Security Act. Hearings before the Committee on Finance, United States Senate, Seventy-Fourth Congress, First Session, on S. 1130, a Bill to Alleviate the Hazards of Old Age, Unemployment, Illness, and Dependency,* vol. 2 (Washington, DC: U.S. Govt. Print. Off., 1935), 485–87.

177 M. S. Venkataramani, "Norman Thomas, Arkansas Sharecroppers, and the Roosevelt Agricultural Policies, 1933–1937," *Journal of American History* 47, no. 2 (September 1960): 225–46, https://academic.oup.com/jah/article-abstract/47/2/225/844826?redirectedFrom=fulltext.

178 "Government to Spend 350 Million to Care for Folks Driven from Land," *The Enid Events,* March 29, 1934, 2.

179 Charles C. Bolton, "Farmers Without Land: The Plight of White Tenant Farmers and Sharecroppers," Mississippi History Now, March 2004, http://mshistorynow.mdah.state.ms.us/articles/228/farmers-without-land-the-plight-of-white-tenant-farmers-and-sharecroppers.

180 David Eugene Conrad, "The Forgotten Farmers: the AAA and the Southern Tenants, 1933-36" (dissertation, University of Illinois Press, 1965), 112–13, https://shareok.org/bitstream/handle/11244/1583/6204121.PDF?sequence=1.

181 Conrad, 115–16.

182 Conrad, 116.

183 United States Congress Committee, *Economic Security Act.*

184 United States Congress Committee, *Economic Security Act.*

185 Theodore E. Whiting, *Final Statistical Report of the Federal Emergency Relief Administration,* Federal Works Agency (Washington, DC: U.S. Government Printing Office, 1942), iii.

186 Castro and Willingham, "Progressive Governance."

187 Conrad, "The Forgotten Farmers," 219.

188 Conrad, 219.

189 Conrad, 220.

190 "The Great Depression Interviews: Interview with Clay East," *The Great Depression Series,* Washington University Libraries, Film and Media Archive, Henry Hampton Collection, September 26, 1992, http://digital.wustl.edu/cgi/t/text/text-idx?c=gds;cc=gds;rgn=-

main;view=text;idno=eas00031.00213.030.

191 Conrad, "The Forgotten Farmers," 123.

192 Paul R. Grabiel, "4 Negroes, One White Man, Killed," *Arkansas Democrat*, October 2, 1919, 1.

193 Francine Uenuma, "The Massacre of Black Sharecroppers That Led the Supreme Court to Curb the Racial Disparities of the Justice System," *Smithsonian Magazine*, August 2, 2018, https://www.smithsonianmag.com/history/death-hundreds-elaine-massacre-led-supreme-court-take-major-step-toward-equal-justice-african-americans-180969863/.

194 Uenuma.

195 Jason Manthorne, "The View from the Cotton: Reconsidering the Southern Tenant Farmers' Union," *Agricultural History* 84, no. 1 (2010): 20–45, http://www.jstor.org/stable/40607621.

196 Robert H. Brown, "New Deal Put to New Test as Southern Share-Cropper Fights Landlords in Court," *The Morning Call*, February 9, 1935, 2.

197 *Labor Unionism in American Agriculture* (Washington, DC: Government Print Office, 1945), 16.

198 *Labor Unionism in American Agriculture*, 16.

199 *Labor Unionism in American Agriculture*, 294.

200 *Labor Unionism in American Agriculture*, 19.

201 *Labor Unionism in American Agriculture*, 294.

202 *Labor Unionism in American Agriculture*, 294.

203 *Labor Unionism in American Agriculture*, 294.

204 Robin D. G. Kelley, *Hammer and Hoe: Alabama Communists During the Great Depression* (Chapel Hill, NC: University of North Carolina Press, 2015), 227.

205 *Labor Unionism in American Agriculture*, 298.

206 "Norman Thomas Takes Up Cause of Share-Cropper," *St. Louis Post-Dispatch*, February 18, 1934, 6.

207 Norman Thomas, "Slum Dweller Lives Better Than Cropper," *American Guardian*, March 9, 1934, 1.

208 "Social Service Plan to Get 1936 Study," *Fort Worth Star-Telegram*,

May 20, 1935, 18.

209 "Slavery and Inhumanity to Sharecroppers," *Lincoln Herald*, March 1, 1935, 1.

210 Associated Press, "Tenant Union Leaders Hiding," *Greenwood Commonwealth*, March 23, 1935, 1.

211 Associated Press, "2 Beaten In Arkansas," *Shreveport Journal*, February 2, 1935, 1.

212 Peter Parley Jr., "A View of the 'Desperate' Problems and Conditions of the Cotton Country," *The Baltimore Sun*, September 3, 1936, 12.

213 Associated Press, "Tenant-Landlord Conflict Marked by Death's Hand," *Dothan Eagle*, March 30, 1935, 1.

214 Reed Hynds, "'Revolt Among Sharecroppers' Pictures Woes of Southern Poor," *St. Louis Star & Times*, March 23, 1936, 13.

215 Hynds.

216 Pamela Browning, "The Decline of Black Farming in America: A Report of the United States Commission on Civil Rights," 1982, iii.

217 "Equal Opportunity in Farm Programs: Excerpts from an Appraisal of Services Rendered by Agencies of the United States Department of Agriculture," 1965, 8.

218 Browning, "The Decline of Black Farming," 10.

219 Browning, 10–11.

220 Browning, iv.

221 Browning, 8–9.

222 Browning, 11.

223 Browning, 69.

224 Browning, 99.

225 Browning, 50.

226 Browning, 50.

227 Browning, 54.

228 Browning, 54.

229 Browning, 60.

230 Browning, 60.

231 Browning, 61–62.

232 Browning, 63.

233 Browning, 64.

234 Browning, 64.

235 Browning, 64.

236 Browning, 66.

237 Browning, 66.

238 Browning, 67.

239 Browning, 73–74.

240 Browning, 71.

241 Browning, 74–75.

242 Browning, 80.

243 Browning, 80.

244 Browning, 81.

245 Browning, 85.

246 Joan Oleck, "Irregularities Found in U.S. Loans to Black Farmers," *News and Observer*, October 27, 1981, 22.

247 Oleck.

248 Oleck.

249 Will Sullivan, "Blacks Charge FmHA Discrimination," *Clarion-Ledger*, December 2, 1979, 3.

250 Browning, "The Decline of Black Farming," 92.

251 Browning, 93.

252 Browning, 93–94.

253 Associated Press, "FmHA Officials Meet with Farmers," *Hattiesburg American*, March 15, 1981, 7.

254 Associated Press, "Black Farmer Charges Loan Discrimination," *Greenwood Commonwealth*, March 17, 1981, 9.

255 Associated Press, "Black Farmers Say FmHA Sit-in Is Ending," *The Jackson Sun*, April 2, 1981.

256 "Gary Grant Interview," August 17, 2011, Interview number U-0773, Southern Oral History Program Collection (#4007), Southern Historical Collection, Louis Round Wilson Special Collections Library, UNC-Chapel Hill, https://dc.lib.unc.edu/cdm/compoundobject/collection/sohp/id/18029/rec/1.

257 "Gary Grant Interview," August 6, 2003, Interview number U-0466,

Southern Oral History Program Collection (#4007), Southern Historical Collection, Louis Round Wilson Special Collections Library,
UNC-Chapel Hill, https://dc.lib.unc.edu/cdm/compoundobject/col-
lection/sohp/id/6197/rec/1.

258 Nash Halifax, "Edgecombe Residents Come Together Monday for
MLK Day Ceremony," *Daily Herald*, 2020.

259 Gary R Grant, "BFAA-The Black Farmers and Agriculturalists
Association," *BFAA-The Black Farmers and Agriculturalists Association*
(blog) (Black Farmers and Agriculturalists Association, April 17,
2009), http://bfaa-us.blogspot.com/.

260 Grant interview, August 17, 2011.

261 Gary R Grant, "BFAA-The Black Farmers and Agriculturalists
Association," *BFAA-The Black Farmers and Agriculturalists Association*
(blog) (Black Farmers and Agriculturalists Association, April 17,
2009), http://bfaa-us.blogspot.com/.

262 C-SPAN, "Agriculture Department Loan Discrimination," C-SPAN,
April 23, 1997, https://www.c-span.org/video/?80632-1/agricul-
ture-department-loan-discrimination.

263 C-SPAN, "Agriculture Department Loan Discrimination."

264 C-SPAN, "Agriculture Department Loan Discrimination."

265 Avis Thomas-Lester, "Farmer Fights to Leave Estate to Next Gen,"
Afro News, June 22, 2016, https://afro.com/farmer-fights-to-leave-es-
tate-to-next-gen/.

266 Associated Press, "Small-time Farmer Becomes a National Figure:
John Boyd Hits Campaign Trail," *Daily Press*, October 1, 2000.

267 Localish, "How Black Farmers Are Being Erased from America's
Agricultural Industry," ABC, July 10, 2020, https://abc.com/shows/
more-in-common/episode-guide/season-01/734-how-black-farmers-
are-being-erased-from-americas-agricultural-industry.

268 Tavis Smiley, "Interview: John Boyd Jr. Discusses His Ride to Washington in a Mule-Drawn Carriage to Proclaim the Plight of Black
Farmers," NPR, November 4, 2003.

269 "Farmer John Boyd Jr. Wants African-Americans to Reconnect with
Farming," NPR, *The Salt*, February 14, 2016.

270 Associated Press, "Small-time Farmer."

271 "Black Farmers Receive Settlement Over Alleged Discrimination Claims," NPR, *Tell Me More*, February 19, 2010).

272 "Black Farmers Receive Settlement Over Alleged Discrimination Claims."

273 "Farmer John Boyd Jr. Wants African-Americans to Reconnect with Farming."

274 "A Quest to be Heard; What Drives a Black Farmer to Work His Fields and the Halls of Congress?" *The Washington Post*, June 21, 2009.

275 Ayana Jones, "Study: Black Pa. Farms in 1800s Thrived, Unlike Today," *Philadelphia Tribune*, February 8, 2011.

276 Mary Beausoleil, "U.S. Farm Agency Acknowledges Bias; Black Group Plans Protest in Washington," *The Richmond Times-Dispatch*, November 30, 1996.

277 Allen G. Breed, "Four Years After Landmark Settlement, Black Farmers Still Fighting Government," Associated Press Archive, August 30, 2002.

278 Edward Martin, "For Land's Sake," *Business North Carolina* 18, no. 11 (November 1, 1998).

279 "Civil Rights Enforcement Record of the Department of Agriculture," serial no. 122, United States Congress House Committee on the Judiciary Subcommittee on Civil and Constitutional Rights (US Printing Office, 1986), https://books.google.com/books?id=vT7r-4JEN6EQC&pg=PA67&lpg=PA67&dq=%22tim%2Bpig-ford%22%2B%22house%2Bjudiciary%2Bsubcommittee%22&-source=bl&ots=v6CPrl8Brk&sig=ACfU3U1FbhVKLeS.

280 Martin, "For Land's Sake."

281 Martin.

282 Martin.

283 "Civil Rights Enforcement Record."

284 Martin, "For Land's Sake."

285 Martin.

286 "Civil Rights Enforcement Record."

287 Martin, "For Land's Sake."

288 "Civil Rights Enforcement Record."

289 "Civil Rights Enforcement Record."

290 "Civil Rights Enforcement Record."

291 "Civil Rights Enforcement Record."

292 "Civil Rights Enforcement Record."

293 "Civil Rights Enforcement Record."

294 "Civil Rights Enforcement Record."

295 Martin, "For Land's Sake."

296 Martin.

297 Jean Pagel, "Black Farmer Reaps Crop of USDA Confusion, Denials," *Miami Herald*, February 1, 1994, 126.

298 Pagel, 126.

299 Pagel, 126.

300 Pagel, 126.

301 Pagel, 126.

302 Williams v. Glickman, 1995 U.S. Dist. LEXIS 13007 (D.D.C. June 6, 1995).

303 Associated Press, "USDA Faces Lawsuit Charging Racial Bias," *Paris News*, March 16, 1994, 9.

304 Associated Press, 9.

305 Associated Press, 9.

306 Associated Press, 9.

307 Williams v. Glickman.

308 Williams v. Glickman.

309 Associated Press, "West Texas Farmer Settles Racial Discrimination Suit," *Austin American-Statesman*, October 23, 1997, 30.

310 Associated Press, 30.

311 "Status on the Implementation of the *Pigford v. Glickman* Settlement: Hearing before the Subcommittee on the Constitution of the Committee on the Judiciary House of Representatives," 108th Cong. 18, September 28, 2004, testimony of Alexander Pires, https://www.govinfo.gov/content/pkg/CHRG-108hhrg96110/html/CHRG-108hhrg96110.htm.

312 Pigford v. Glickman, 1997 U.S. Dist. PACER 1:97-cv-01978-PLF

(D.D.C. August 28, 1997).

313 Pigford v. Glickman.

314 Pamela Stallsmith, "Ignored Since '83, Complaints Will Need New Investigations," *Richmond Times-Dispatch*, May 25, 1997.

315 Pamela Stallsmith, "No More Sitting In Back of the Bus: Lloyd Wright Tackling 'Subtle' Discrimination," *Richmond Times-Dispatch*, May 25, 1997.

316 Peter Hardin, "Review Finds Racial Bias Inside USDA; Team Suggests Series of Corrective Steps," *Richmond Times-Dispatch*, February 28, 1997, A-1.

317 Hardin.

318 Hardin.

319 Pigford v. Glickman. [[appears to be this—confirm? YES]]

320 Peter Scott, "Black Farmers Suing for Bias Are Offered Deal," *Atlanta Journal-Constitution*, November 24, 1998, 3A.

321 David Firestone, "Agriculture Dept. to Settle Lawsuit by Black Farmers," *The New York Times*, January 5, 1999, 1, https://www.nytimes.com/1999/01/05/us/agriculture-dept-to-settle-lawsuit-by-black-farmers.html.

322 Associated Press, "Judge Approves Settlement for Black Farmers," *The New York Times*, April 15, 1999, https://www.nytimes.com/1999/04/15/us/judge-approves-settlement-for-black-farmers.html.

323 Firestone, "Agriculture Dept. to Settle Lawsuit."

324 Associated Press, "Judge Approves Settlement."

325 Opinion, Pigford v. Glickman, United States District Court, District of Columbia, April 14, 1999, 185 F.R.D. 82 (D.D.C. 1999).

326 Opinion, Pigford v. Glickman.

327 Opinion, Pigford v. Glickman.

328 Opinion, Pigford v. Glickman.

329 Opinion, Pigford v. Glickman.

330 Opinion, Pigford v. Glickman.

331 Opinion, Pigford v. Glickman.

332 Opinion, Pigford v. Glickman.

333 Gary R. Grant, "A Real Look at the Pigford vs. Glickman," Black

Farmers & Agriculturalists Association, April 17, 2009, http://bfaa-us.blogspot.com/2009/04/real-look-at-pigford-vs-glickman.html.

334 "Status on the Implementation of the *Pigford v. Glickman* Settlement: Hearing before the Subcommittee on the Constitution, of the Committee on the Judiciary House of Representatives," 108th Cong. 18, September 28, 2004, testimony of Randi Roth, https://www.govinfo.gov/content/pkg/CHRG-108hhrg96110/html/CHRG-108hhrg96110.htm.

335 "Status on the Implementation of the *Pigford v. Glickman* Settlement," testimony of Randi Roth.

336 "Status on the Implementation of the *Pigford v. Glickman* Settlement: Hearing before the Subcommittee on the Constitution, of the Committee on the Judiciary House of Representatives," 108th Cong. 18, September 28, 2004, testimony of Michael K. Lewis, https://www.govinfo.gov/content/pkg/CHRG-108hhrg96110/html/CHRG-108hhrg96110.htm.

337 "Status on the Implementation of the *Pigford v. Glickman* Settlement," testimony of Michael K. Lewis.

338 "Status on the Implementation of the *Pigford v. Glickman* Settlement," testimony of Michael K. Lewis.

339 "'Notice' Provision in the *Pigford v. Glickman* Consent Decree: Hearing before the Subcommittee on the Constitution, of the Committee on the Judiciary House of Representatives," 108th Cong. 18 (2004), exhibit, 280.

340 Mary Orndorff, "Black Farmers' Discrimination Case Slows, Payments Denied 40 Percent of Claims Rejected; Alabama has Highest Approval Rate in South with 69 Percent," *The Birmingham News*, July 20, 2004.

341 Amy Lotven, "Black Farmers Group to Protest at USDA," *The Daily Herald*, April 27, 2006.

342 "'Notice' Provision in the *Pigford v. Glickman* Consent Decree," Hearing before the Subcommittee on the Constitution, of the Committee on the Judiciary House of Representatives," 108th Cong. 18 (2004), testimony of Steve Chabot.

343 "'Notice' Provision in the *Pigford v. Glickman* Consent Decree," testi-

mony of Steve Chabot.

344 "'Notice' Provision in the *Pigford v. Glickman* Consent Decree: Hearing before the Subcommittee on the Constitution, of the Committee on the Judiciary House of Representatives," 108th Cong. 18 (2004), testimony of J.L. Chestnut.

345 "'Notice' Provision in the *Pigford v. Glickman* Consent Decree: Hearing before the Subcommittee on the Constitution, of the Committee on the Judiciary House of Representatives," 108th Cong. 18 (2004), testimony of Jeanne C. Finegan.

346 "'Notice' Provision in the *Pigford v. Glickman* Consent Decree," testimony of Jeanne C. Finegan.

347 "'Notice' Provision in the *Pigford v. Glickman* Consent Decree," testimony of Jeanne C. Finegan.

348 "'Notice' Provision in the *Pigford v. Glickman* Consent Decree," testimony of Jeanne C. Finegan.

349 "'Notice' Provision in the *Pigford v. Glickman* Consent Decree," testimony of Jeanne C. Finegan.

350 "'Notice' Provision in the *Pigford v. Glickman* Consent Decree: Hearing before the Subcommittee on the Constitution, of the Committee on the Judiciary House of Representatives," 108th Cong. 18 (2004), testimony of Thomas Burrell.

351 "'Notice' Provision in the *Pigford v. Glickman* Consent Decree," testimony of Thomas Burrell.

352 "'Notice' Provision in the *Pigford v. Glickman* Consent Decree," testimony of Thomas Burrell.

353 "Status on the Implementation of the *Pigford v. Glickman* Settlement: Hearing before the Subcommittee on the Constitution, of the Committee on the Judiciary House of Representatives," 108th Cong. 18, September 28, 2004, testimony of Phillip J. Haynie II, https://www.govinfo.gov/content/pkg/CHRG-108hhrg96110/html/CHRG-108hhrg96110.htm.

354 "Status on the Implementation of the *Pigford v. Glickman* Settlement," testimony of Phillip J. Haynie II.

355 "Status on the Implementation of the *Pigford v. Glickman* Settlement," testimony of Phillip J. Haynie II.

356 "Status on the Implementation of the *Pigford v. Glickman* Settlement," testimony of Phillip J. Haynie II.

357 "Status on the Implementation of the *Pigford v. Glickman* Settlement," testimony of Phillip J. Haynie II.

358 "Status on the Implementation of the *Pigford v. Glickman* Settlement," testimony of Phillip J. Haynie II.

359 Ana Radelat, "Farm Bill Would Give Black Farmers 2nd Chance," *Gannett News Service,* January 7, 2008.

360 "Agriculture," Espy for Senate website, accessed February 15, 2021, https://espyforsenate.com/issues/agriculture

361 Karen Tumulty, "Five Blacks in South Given Chance in House Elections," *Los Angeles Times*, October 29, 1986.

362 James R. Dickenson, "House Rivals Tread Fine Line in Race-Conscious Mississippi," *The Washington Post*, October 29, 1986.

363 "The Elections: Out with the Old; The Voters Pluck Some New Faces from the Political Crowd: Governors," *The New York Times*, November 6, 1986.

364 Marshall Ingwerson, "In Deepest of Deep South, Black Lawmaker Wins Many Whites," *The Christian Science Monitor*, October 21, 1988, https://www.csmonitor.com/1988/1021/aespy.html.

365 Bartholomew Sullivan, "Black farmers, Including from the Mid-South, Tell Judge USDA Settlement is Flawed," *Commercial Appeal*, Tribune Content Agency, September 2, 2011.

366 Khalil Abdullah, "Espy's Path to the U.S. Senate Includes Black, White and 'Purple People' of Mississippi," *Mississippi Link*, November 1, 2018.

367 Abdullah.

368 Abdullah.

369 Charles Conner, "Black Farmers Suing USDA Recruit Others Claiming Bias," *Commercial Appeal*, February 4, 1998.

370 William E. Clayton Jr., "Espy Indicted on 39 Counts/Ex-USDA Chief Charged with Taking Gifts, Cover-up," *Houston Chronicle*, August 28, 1997.

371 Conner, "Black Farmers Suing USDA."

372 Ellyn Ferguson, "Espy: Clinton Administration Must Speed Up Ac-

tion on Black Farmers' Complaints," *USA Today*, September 23, 1997.

373 Ferguson.

374 Mary Ann Akers, "Espy Corruption Case Goes to Federal Jury—
Gifts Didn't Affect Policy, Defense Team Says," *The Washington
Times*, December 1, 1998.

375 "Former Cabinet Member Cleared of All 30 Charges," *St. Petersburg
Times*, December 3, 1998.

376 Francis X. Clines, "Joyful in Victory, Espy is Mindful of Price," *The
New York Times*, December 3, 1998.

377 Erin France, "Black Farmers Could Still Lay Claim to Restitution,"
Pine Bluff Commercial, Arkansas Democrat-Gazette, October 12, 2008.

378 France.

379 Barack Obama, "Statement by the President on the Court Approval
of the Settlement of the Black Farmers Lawsuit," National Archives
and Records Administration, October 28, 2011, https://obamawhite-
house.archives.gov/the-press-office/2011/10/28/statement-presi-
dent-court-approval-settlement-black-farmers-lawsuit.

380 Barack Obama.

381 Ira Berlin, *The Making of African America: The Four Great Migrations*
(New York, NY: Penguin, 2011).

382 Berlin.

383 Berlin.

384 "Booker, Warren, Gillibrand Announce Comprehensive Bill to Address the History of Discrimination in Federal Agricultural Policy,"
Cory Booker website, November 19, 2020, https://www.booker.
senate.gov/news/press/-booker-warren
-gillibrand-announce-comprehensive-bill-to-address-the-histo-
ry-of-discrimination-in-federal-agricultural-policy.

385 Julie Rose, "Black Farmers Must Keep Waiting for Bias Settlement,"
NPR, *Morning Edition*, March 30, 2010.

386 "Eighth Amended Class Action Complaint," case number
1:99CV03119, United States District Court for the District of
Columbia, Civil Rights Litigation Clearinghouse, February 11, 2008,
https://www.clearinghouse.net/chDocs/public/FH-DC-0009-0001.
pdf

387 Ben Jealous, "First Black Farmers Lawsuit Can't Be Last," *Philadelphia Tribune*, May 19, 2013.

388 Dan Glickman and Tom Vilsack, "Commentary: Black Farmers and the USDA: Lessons for the Black Lives Matter Movement," *Chicago Tribune*, August 14, 2020.

389 "House Agriculture Committee Hearing on the State of the Rural Economy," Political Transcript Wire, February 7, 2018.

390 "The Biden-Harris Plan to Build Back Better in Rural America," JoeBiden.com, accessed February 15, 2021, https://joebiden.com/rural-plan/.

391 Hiroko Tabuchi and Nadja Popovich, "Two Biden Priorities, Climate and Inequality, Meet on Black-Owned Farms," *The New York Times*, January 31, 2021, https://www.nytimes.com/2021/01/31/climate/black-farmers-discrimination-agriculture.html .

392 Peter O'Dowd and Allison Hagan, "Black Farmers Disappointed in Biden's Pick for Secretary of Agriculture," WBUR, *Here & Now*, January 5, 2021, https://www.wbur.org/hereandnow/2021/01/05/black-farmers-biden-vilsack.

393 "Booker, Warren, Gillibrand."

394 "Booker, Warren, Gillibrand."

395 "Booker, Warren, Gillibrand."

396 Glickman and Vilsack, "Commentary."